Problem Solving and the FAE

4th Edition

Derry Cotter

Published in 2019 by
Chartered Accountants Ireland
Chartered Accountants House
47 – 49 Pearse Street
Dublin 2

www.charteredaccountants.ie

ISBN: 978-1-912350-33-9

Typeset by Datapage
Printed by Replika Press Pvt. Ltd.

MIX
Paper from
responsible sources
FSC
www.fsc.org   FSC® C016779

This book is dedicated to my sister Mary

To FAE students – may you find a solution to every problem

CONTENTS

Introduction

Most of us have difficulty recalling our first exposure to tasks that involved problem solving. This is because our first experience of problem solving was as babies, when we learned to insert plastic or wooden pieces into different shaped openings. I have a vivid memory of my son, at age three, identifying a momentous problem on our return home from a family outing.

"How did you get the house in through the gate?" he asked, sizing up the difficulty of the problem as he saw it. The question prompted his parents to quickly acquire a supply of Lego as a problem-solving tool. It must have worked, because he never asked the question again!

As adults our education in problem solving continued with super sleuth, Sherlock Holmes, another problem-solving master. Dismissing the observations of his sidekick, Dr Watson, Holmes invariably solved the most baffling of mysteries. Agatha Christie gave us Miss Marple and Hercule Poirot, and we have often marvelled at the problem-solving skills of Inspector Morse, John Rebus, Kojak and the unassuming Lieutenant Columbo.

The master playwright, Shakespeare, was no slouch when it came to problem solving and, in *Hamlet,* the bard demonstrates the power of a play within a play. Suspecting that his uncle is responsible for his father's murder, Hamlet engages a travelling troupe of actors to re-enact the crime. As planned, his uncle's innocence is duly blown, his demeanour betraying a conscience racked by guilt.

Chartered Accountants Ireland's Final Admitting Exam (the 'FAE') presents aspiring Chartered Accountants with a problem within a problem. The ultimate challenge or problem is how to pass the FAE and, to succeed, candidates must solve a selection of carefully chosen problems posed by FAE examiners. The challenge for the examiner is to establish which students achieve competence in the FAE. To achieve **competence** you must satisfy two fundamental criteria as outlined in **Figure 1**.

FIGURE 1: ACHIEVING COMPETENCE IN THE **FAE**

Mastery of Business Knowledge

Members of a professional body are assumed to be proficient in their chosen area of expertise. Thus, medical practitioners should have a detailed knowledge of the human body and of illnesses that can affect it. Lawyers are expected to be familiar with legal principles and with relevant case law. Engineers are experts in assessing structural issues relating to buildings.

Similarly, a Chartered Accountant is **expected to have a sound understanding of how business works**. It is for this reason that the FAE evaluates students across a broad spectrum of subject areas. A successful FAE student will have a skill set akin to that of a general medical practitioner. He/she will possess the knowledge to assist clients with issues involving areas as diverse as financial accounting and reporting, management accounting, finance, audit and assurance, strategic management and leadership, risk management and sustainability, tax planning and the use of data analytics, artificial intelligence and other emerging technologies.

A general practitioner can, of course, choose to specialise in areas such as paediatrics, surgery, geriatrics or palliative care. This type of specialist knowledge is also expected of an aspiring Chartered Accountant. Thus, in addition to proving proficiency in general business matters, an FAE student must demonstrate **detailed knowledge of a specific subject area**. These are the FAE's 'Elective' options, of which there are currently five to choose from: Advanced Auditing and Assurance, Advisory, Advanced Taxation, Financial Services and Public Sector.

From a problem-solving perspective, therefore, the task of an FAE student is similar to that facing a contestant in the hit quiz show, *Mastermind*. Here, each contestant is posed a range of general questions as well as ones on his/her chosen specialist subject.

Acquiring an advanced level of technical knowledge is therefore of critical importance for the FAE student. Thus, it is essential to fully **understand** the technical content of areas such as international financial reporting standards, auditing standards, tax planning options, etc. The more that you know and understand about areas such as these, the more your ability to perform in the FAE will be enhanced. Although the FAE is examined on an open-book basis, it will not be feasible to acquire this knowledge during the examination. You just won't have the time to locate material and go through it.

So, throughout the FAE Course Programme, invest as much time as possible in developing your technical knowledge. In this context, the **single-discipline lectures** are a key element in ensuring that your technical knowledge is at a sufficiently advanced level in individual subject disciplines. *Note:* the FAE Competency Statement, which is published online annually, is the Institute's syllabus and a very important point of reference for students.

It is also essential to stress that knowledge entails understanding. Learning by rote is not a productive activity and, in an open-book examination, it will be of little or no benefit. So, try to gain an understanding of each area that you study. This is a prerequisite for effective problem solving.

Application of Knowledge

Applying one's knowledge in a relevant way is the single most important FAE skill. To achieve competence, it is essential to address the specifics of each FAE case. Should a patient present with a severe stomach pain, for example, there is little point in a medical practitioner treating other ailments such as a sprained ankle or a sore ear. The urgency of the matter demands an immediate investigation of the patient's acute stomach symptoms. The cause of the pain must be identified and treatment administered without delay.

Similarly, when an FAE student is asked to solve a business problem, **he must be completely focused on the issue at hand**. For example, a business may be in danger of becoming insolvent due to having to service an unaffordable level of debt repayments. There is little point in suggesting that the business should improve its working capital management or that it should curtail its dividend payments. Both are laudable suggestions, but they fail to address the entity's imminent bankruptcy. **What is needed is for the business to reschedule its repayments by extending the term of its loans**. Refinancing itself in this way reduces its short-term commitments, thus providing the business with an opportunity to restore its financial health. Supplementary measures, such as improved working capital management and a suspension of dividend payments may then be proposed as additional coping mechanisms.

It should be remembered that, in an open-book format, an examiner will not reward a student for regurgitating material from readily accessible sources. General points relating to achieving improved liquidity are of little value when a firm's debt burden is about to render it bankrupt. **Instead, a competent student will address the fundamental problem of the entity's debt commitments, and suggest how these could be refinanced**.

Summary

Demonstrating competence is the core requirement for success in the FAE. This requires that successful candidates show themselves to be effective problem solvers. Armed with the requisite level of knowledge, a professional has the potential to achieve competence in his/her chosen field. Ultimately, however, the realisation of this potential requires that **knowledge is skilfully applied to identify specific solutions for specific problems**.

Acknowledgements

I wish to thank Ronan O'Loughlin for recommending that this book be published, and Michael Diviney for commissioning it.

Thanks too to John Munnelly in the Examinations Department at Chartered Accountants Ireland and to Liam Boyle and the editing and design team for their invaluable assistance.

I am also indebted to my family for their ongoing support and encouragement.

PART I

Structure and Assessment of the FAE

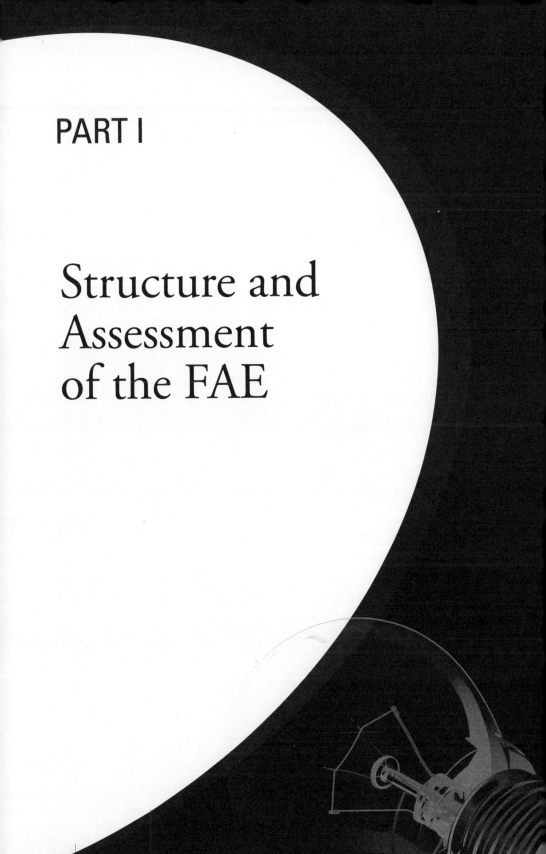

Chapter 1. Structure of the FAE

The FAE consists of two components:

1. FAE Core:
   - ■ Paper 1
   - ■ Interim assessment – Advanced Application of Financial Reporting Principles (AAFRP)

   and

2. FAE Elective:
   - ■ Paper 2 – at the end of the year
   - ■ Interim assessment

The content of each of these areas is now outlined in detail.

FAE Core

Paper 1

Paper 1 consists of a single 4-hour case study (plus 30 minutes reading time), which requires students to have an understanding of a broad spectrum of business modules. The specific modules are subject to change and students should refer to the FAE Competency Statement for their given year, which can be accessed at www.charteredaccountants.ie. Currently, there are four business modules:

1. Financial Reporting
2. Strategic Management and Leadership
3. Data Analytics, Artificial Intelligence and Emerging Technologies
4. Risk Management and Sustainability.

Students should refer to the FAE Competency Statement for the weighting of these subject areas.

The paper contains approximately **eight to ten primary indicators**, which equates to **eight to ten individual issues that must be addressed in the case study**. For example, a candidate may identify the formulation of a strategic plan for a company as an important issue. This would constitute one indicator.

A candidate's result in Paper 1 counts as 85% of FAE Core.

Interim Assessment – AAFRP

Advanced Application of Financial Reporting Principles (AAFRP) assesses a candidate's technical ability, judgement and decision-making abilities in double-entry accounting, presentation of financial information and financial reporting disclosure. A candidate's result in the AAFRP assessment **counts as 15% of FAE Core.**

FAE Elective

All candidates must complete one FAE Elective module. Currently, candidates can choose from the following options:
■ Advanced Auditing and Assurance
■ Advisory
■ Advanced Taxation (NI or ROI variant)
■ Financial Services
■ Public Sector.

Again, students should refer to the Competency Statement for the module options available to them in any given year.

A candidate's chosen elective is examined by the following.
■ Paper 2, a 4-hour (plus 30 minutes reading time) end-of-year examination. This paper comprises two case studies, each containing four to five primary indicators. Paper 2 is worth 85% of the overall FAE Elective.
■ An interim assessment worth 15% of the overall FAE Elective. The interim assessment is scenario based, and it comprises three to four issues.

Summary

The FAE consists of the FAE Core and the FAE Elective.

FAE Core comprises Paper 1, which requires coverage of all of the business modules as outlined in the Competency Statement, and the AAFRP interim assessment on financial reporting.

FAE Elective requires candidates to choose one subject area as outlined in the Competency Statement. The FAE Elective is examined by Paper 2 of the end-of-year examinations and an interim assessment.

Chapter 2. Assessment of the FAE

Introduction

The FAE Core Paper 1 accounts for 85% of the overall result for FAE Core. The AAFRP interim assessment makes up the remaining 15% of FAE Core.

The FAE Elective end-of-year exam (i.e. Paper 2) counts for 85% of the overall result for FAE Elective. The interim assessment makes up the remaining 15% of FAE Elective.

FAE Core

To pass FAE Core, a candidate must obtain a minimum weighted-average mark of 50% when the marks for Paper 1 and the AAFRP interim assessment are combined.

Paper 1

As outlined in **Chapter 1**, the FAE Core Paper 1 consists of a case study based around a number of key business issues (i.e. 'indicators').

Paper 1 comprises a total of 8–10 indicators. Each indicator is assessed using a combination of:
- a traditional marking approach (e.g. marks for various requirement as in CAP 1 or CAP 2). This will count for 75–85% of the total marks available for each indicator; **and**
- professional competency – marks are awarded on a five-point scale (see **Appendix 2.3** below). This will count for 15–25% of the total marks available for each indicator.

AAFRP Interim Assessment

A traditional marking approach is used, and this assessment makes up 15% of the total marks available in FAE Core.

An example of the assessment of FAE Core is outlined in **Appendix 2.1** below.

FAE Elective

To pass the FAE Elective, a candidate must obtain a minimum weighted-average mark of 50% when the marks for Paper 2 and the interim assessment are combined.

Paper 2

As outlined in **Chapter 1**, Paper 2 comprises two case studies. These case studies are based around a number of key business issues (i.e. 'indicators').

Paper 2 contains a total of 8–9 indicators. Each indicator is assessed using a combination of:

■ a traditional marking approach (e.g. marks for various requirements as in CAP 1 or CAP 2). This will count for 75–85% of the total marks available for each indicator; **and**

■ professional competency – marks are awarded on a five-point scale (see **Appendix 2.3** below). This will count for 15–25% of the total marks available for each indicator.

Interim Assessment

As outlined in **Chapter 1**, the interim assessment consists of one case study containing three to four issues. Each issue is assessed using a combination of:

■ a traditional-marking approach (e.g. marks for various requirement as in CAP 1 or CAP 2). This will count for 75–85% of the total marks available for each issue; **and**

■ professional competency – marks are awarded on a five-point scale (see **Appendix 2.3** below). This will count for 15–25% of the total marks available for each issue.

An example of the assessment of FAE Elective is outlined in **Appendix 2.2** below.

Appendix 2.1: **Example of Assessment of FAE Core**

(a) Paper 1

In this example assume there are eight indicators altogether across the Core Paper 1. Each indicator has an equal weighting and assume each indicator is worth 100 marks.

Say an indicator relates to research and development expenditure, and requires a candidate to provide:
- the appropriate accounting treatment in accordance with IFRS (50 marks);
- the journal entries in accordance with IFRS (30 marks); and
- professional competency (20 marks).

Assume that Candidate A achieves the following marks for this indicator:
- 20 marks for the accounting treatment;
- 16 marks for the journal entries; and
- 12 marks for professional competency.

Candidate A will therefore have achieved 48% of the available marks in this indicator.

Candidate A obtains an average mark of 64% in respect of the other seven indicators. Candidate A's mark for Paper 1 is then computed as follows:

$(48\% \times 1/8) + (64\% \times 7/8) = 62\%$

As Paper 1 counts for 85% of FAE Core, Candidate A will have earned the following mark towards the overall assessment of FAE Core:

$62\% \times 85\% =$ **52.7%**

(b) AAFRP Interim Assessment

Assume that Candidate A achieved a mark of 40% in this assessment. As the AAFRP interim assessment counts for 15% of FAE Core, Candidate A will have earned the following additional mark towards the overall assessment of FAE Core:

$40\% \times 15\% =$ **6%**

(c) Overall Assessment of FAE Core

Candidate A's overall mark for FAE Core is computed by adding together the marks from Paper 1 and the AAFRP interim assessment. This gives a total mark of 58.7% (i.e. 52.7% + 6%). Having satisfied the minimum required mark of 50%, Candidate A has therefore passed FAE Core.

Appendix 2.2: **Example of Assessment of FAE Elective**

(a) Paper 2

In this example, assume that there are eight indicators in total in the end-of-year Elective exam. Each indicator has an equal weighting and assume each indicator is worth 100 marks.

Assume also that we are dealing with the Advanced Audit and Assurance Elective, and that an indicator in this paper relating to a client's internal control system requires a candidate to provide:
■ deficiencies in the existing system (40 marks);
■ improvements that are required (35 marks); and
■ professional competency (25 marks).

Assume that Candidate A achieves the following marks for this indicator:
■ 20 marks for identifying deficiencies of the existing system;
■ 18 marks for identifying the required improvements; and
■ 10 marks for professional competency.

Candidate A will therefore have achieved 48% of the available marks in this indicator.

Candidate A obtains an average mark of 56% in respect of the other seven indicators. Candidate A's mark for Paper 2 is then computed as follows:

$(48\% \times 1/8) + (56\% \times 7/8) = 55\%$

As the Elective exam counts for 85% of FAE Elective, Candidate A will have earned the following mark towards the overall assessment of FAE Elective:

$55\% \times 85\% = \mathbf{46.75\%}$

(b) Interim Assessment

Assume that there are four issues in this scenario-based paper. These issues are assessed using the same marking system as outlined above

Assume that Candidate A obtains an overall average mark of 60% for the four issues. As the interim assessment counts for 15% of the FAE Elective, Candidate A will have earned the following additional mark towards the overall assessment of the FAE Elective:

$60\% \times 15\% = \mathbf{9\%}$

(c) Overall Assessment of the FAE Elective

Candidate A's overall mark for the FAE Elective is computed by adding together the marks from Paper 2 and the interim assessment. This gives a total mark of 55.75% (i.e. 46.75% + 9%). Having achieved the minimum required mark of 50%, Candidate A has therefore passed the FAE Elective.

Appendix 2.3: Professional Competency

Professional competency marks make up 15–25% of the total marks available for each indicator in the following papers:
- FAE Core Paper 1;
- Elective interim assessment; and
- Elective end-of-year exam (i.e. Paper 2).

The Examiner assesses the following criteria in awarding marks for professional competency:
- presentation and layout;
- laying out arguments in a clear, concise and persuasive manner, with robust justifications for points raised;
- demonstrating awareness, using judgement and showing insight;
- investigating, scrutinising and reflecting on key points raised; and
- assessing, estimating and appraising options.

Using the above criteria, a candidate's professional competency mark for each indicator is computed on a five-point scale as summarised in **Figure 2.1**.

FIGURE 2.1: FAE – PROFESSIONAL COMPETENCY MARKING SCALE

Point on Scale	Quality Achieved	Professional Competency Mark
Not addressed (NA)	Indicator not addressed	Zero
Nominal competence (NC)	Little of reasonable value	Zero
Basic competence (BC)	Reasonable/basic	Circa 30% of available mark
Competent (C)	Good	Circa 60% of available mark
Highly competent (HC)	Excellent	Circa 100% of available mark

In **Appendix 2.1** above, Candidate A obtained 60% (i.e. 12 marks out of 20) of the marks available for professional competency. This indicates that Candidate A provided a good quality answer in respect of the criteria (e.g. presentation and layout) used in evaluating professional competence.

PART II

Laying the Foundations

Chapter 3. Maximise your Brain Power

The famous author, Norman Vincent Peale,[1] noted a sign at a petrol station he once visited:

> "A Clean Engine Always Delivers Power."

This is a statement that we would do well to reflect on. Effective problem solving requires our brain to be working at maximum efficiency. Carefully maintained and properly nurtured, it can equally be claimed that "A Focused Brain Always Delivers Power."

We are used to looking after our physical wellbeing and maintaining the things we own. Dental check-ups are a normal part of life, as is the taking of medicines to treat common infections. Our cars get a regular NCT or MOT test to ensure that they are safe and running efficiently. Burglar alarms are routinely serviced, and smoke alarms are tested periodically to check if they are in proper working order.

Strangely, although our brain is constantly called upon to solve a myriad of problems, we spend little, if any, time in maintaining its level of efficiency. In fact, our brain is arguably the most ill-treated part of our body. Often forced to work long hours in unpleasant conditions, it is regularly deprived of the sleep that is essential for its regeneration and recovery. Eventually our thought processes become muddled and our decision-making less efficient – and we wonder why.

Clearly we are not good at providing the care and attention that our brain needs in order to operate efficiently. Mostly we do not notice our under-performance, because our lives tend to involve relatively mundane choices. Whether to walk or take the bus, for example, is normally not a difficult decision. In making such a judgement call, the weather, our desire for exercise and the amount of available time are likely to be factors we would consider.

For professional students, however, the challenges are far more intellectually demanding. In examinations the decision-making criteria are rarely routine. This is particularly true at FAE level, where critical thinking and the ability to exercise judgement are of paramount importance. Problem solving at this level requires one's brain to be functioning at a level of efficiency rarely demanded in everyday life. This is illustrated in **Figure 3.1**.

This chapter focuses on the attributes necessary for one's brain to excel in problem solving. If you are to maximise

FIGURE **3.1**: DECISION-MAKING IN THE **FAE**

- FAE
- Non-routine Decision Making
- Exercise Judgement
- Critical Thinking

---

[1] Peale, N.V. (1974), *You Can if You Think You Can,* Simon & Schuster, New York.

your brain's potential, then concentration is a key factor. Simulating exam-type problems is also an important part of your preparation. Research shows that the brain works most efficiently when it is exposed to a type of problem that it has already solved previously. Attitude is also a factor, and problem solving improves when positive thinking becomes a basic part of one's mindset. Finally, almost anything is possible with perseverance.

These factors are summarised in **Figure 3.2** and the remainder of this chapter examines them in more detail.

FIGURE 3.2: MAXIMISING YOUR BRAIN POWER

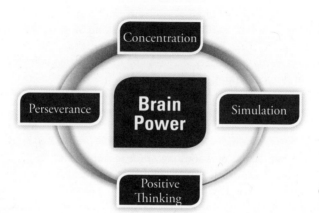

Concentration

When we are 'in the zone', problem solving is easy. Sometimes our brains process information in a way that allows us to identify convincing solutions to complex issues. You can almost hear your brain whirring as it goes about its business and, at times like this, concentration is total. So, what do we need to do to replicate this level of performance on a consistent basis?

Eliminate Interruptions

Research has found that e-mail, mobile phones and Internet usage have an adverse effect on our ability to concentrate. Picture the scene when you are presented with a problem you must solve. As you consider its intricacies, your mobile phone beeps and you divert your attention to answer a friend's text message. A minute later, the screen on your laptop flashes, and you open an e-mail recommending yet another special offer.

This type of repetitive intrusion significantly affects your capacity for problem solving. You are unable to focus sufficiently to absorb a problem's complexities or to formulate potential solutions. Griffey[2] reports the results of a Hewlett-Packard study in which "…62% of adults were addicted to their e-mail to the point where they were checking messages during meetings, after working hours and on holiday". She also refers to the contention of

---

[2] Griffey, H. (2010), *The Art of Concentration*, Rodale, London.

Stafford and Webb[3] that e-mail users are subject to the same learning mechanisms that drive gambling addicts:

> "Rather than reward an action every time it is performed, you reward it sometimes, but not in a predictable way. So with e-mail, usually when I check it there is nothing interesting, but every so often there is something wonderful – an invite out or maybe some juicy gossip – and I get a reward."

Text messages work in a similarly addictive fashion, constantly demanding our attention while adding little of consequence to our lives. So, in order to enable your brain to focus on the task at hand, distance yourself from needless distractions for the duration of your study session. Incidentally, as I write this paragraph I have had to turn off my e-mail to avoid the regular flashes signalling the arrival of new messages.

Relaxation

It is normal to feel stressed when an urgent matter puts you under pressure. Our bodies are programmed to cope with moments like this, and a rush of adrenalin will enable us to deal with the matter. Indeed, the 'fight or flight' type scenario, regularly faced by our cave-dwelling ancestors, continues to confront us from time to time. If anxiety is ongoing, however, it can severely undermine our capacity for problem solving. The brain works best when it is free from external pressures, allowing it to focus completely on the task at hand.

Thus, if you feel under stress for a sustained period of time, you should address the issue. Getting regular physical exercise is important to achieve an overall balance in our lives, and it helps to defuse any stress that has built up in our bodies and minds. Exercise can take the form of jogging or a brisk walk, a swim, a session in the gym or something more competitive for those who are so inclined.

Meditation is also a very effective way of cultivating a relaxed state of mind and sharpening one's intellect. Indeed, the story is told that the Dalai Lama, when informed that he would be extremely busy on a forthcoming tour, was heard to remark that he would have to "meditate even more". Basic meditation (or mindfulness as it is sometimes called) requires that one sit comfortably, eyes closed, and silently recite a mantra, such as a word like *shareem* which has no obvious meaning. Soon, your breathing will become deeper and you will find yourself entering a more relaxed state. Occasionally you will even find yourself falling asleep. A meditation session should typically last about 15–20 minutes and, practised regularly, will greatly improve your concentration and problem-solving abilities.

You should seek medical advice if you find that your stress levels are not reduced by using relaxation techniques or by taking regular exercise.

Sleep

A good night's sleep is a prerequisite for effective problem solving. Tiredness seriously reduces our ability to concentrate; it is often more productive to spend less time studying, enabling you to maintain maximum focus on what you are learning. This is particularly true of an open-book examination, like the FAE, where understanding and application are two of the key objectives.

[3] Stafford, T. & Webb, M. (2004), *Mind Hacks: Tips and Tricks for Using Your Brain*, O'Reilly Media Inc.

Diet

In her excellent book, *The Art of Concentration*, Harriet Griffey[4] deals comprehensively with the connection between diet and brain performance. She outlines how the brain's primary source of energy is glucose, which is derived from carbohydrates digested by the body. Fluctuating glucose levels reduce the brain's ability to work efficiently; and it performs best with a well-regulated supply, which is provided by eating at consistent intervals.

Some foods have a longer digestive period and release glucose more slowly over a sustained period. These are referred to as complex carbohydrates, and they include wholegrain cereals, vegetables, wholemeal pasta, beans and oats. On the other hand, simple carbohydrates, such as sugar, are digested very quickly, leading to peaks and troughs in the supply of glucose to the brain.

Protein intake is also important as it stabilises blood sugar levels and provides amino acids to our brain cells, enabling us to think more clearly. Sources of protein include meat, seafood, eggs, milk, cheese, yoghurt and beans.

Omega 3 fatty acids have also been proven to have a positive effect on brain function. The primary source is oily fish, such as mackerel, herrings, wild salmon and tuna. A fish oil supplement of Omega 3 could also be considered.

Coffee contains caffeine, a stimulant that boosts the production of cortisone and adrenaline. As the brain works best when in a calm state, you should not drink coffee to excess. That's not to say, however, that you shouldn't enjoy the occasional cup of your favourite coffee bean!

Griffey maintains that there are three basic principles regarding food:
- freshness;
- diversity; and
- balance.

So, for efficient brain activity you should have a well-balanced diet, rely less on products that are high in sugar, and eat fresh food as much as possible.

Frequent Study Breaks

Research has shown that the material you study at the beginning and end of a session is what you will remember best. Therefore, a study session of about 45 minutes may be optimal. You should then take a short break before starting back.

Simulation

It takes time for one's brain to adapt to a new situation. When learning to drive, for example, manoeuvres such as reversing or starting on a hill can be challenging. With practice, however, we learn the skills necessary to perform these tasks with minimum difficulty. This is because our brain is at its most efficient when handling problems which it has faced many times before. Repetition reduces the level of difficulty.

---

[4] Griffey, H. (2010), *op. cit.*, above n.4.

In the FAE, mastering the case study technique is a skill that is best acquired throughout your FAE year and into your study leave. Gradually, as your brain adapts to the challenge, you will find yourself completing cases more skilfully and in less time.

It is critical that you spend time working on case studies as this will develop the problem-solving skills that you need in the FAE. On any one day only a very small percentage of what you study is likely to be examined. By attempting case studies, however, you are ensuring that your problem-solving skills become more routine and therefore more efficient.

The importance of practice and experience is evident from the comments of South African rugby player, B.J. Botha:[5]

> "With a little bit of experience … you're more relaxed until you hit the field. At that stage something takes over that you can't explain. You're in your own little world and you can't even hear the crowd … When I was younger you got on the field and you were buzzing. It lasts 10 minutes and then it's over. To work yourself through a game … you need concentration. You can't concentrate when you're in that mental state that you're hyped up and ready to run through a brick wall."

Clearly, concentration improves with practice. That is, as long as you are practising in the right way.

A broad range of practice case material is available to FAE students in any given year. As suggested above, FAE students should work through the relevant case material as a means of acquiring the skills expected of a qualifying Chartered Accountant. This method of study will provide far greater benefits than merely reading suggested solutions.

Positive Thinking

You Can if You Think You Can is the title of Norman Vincent Peale's[6] best-selling book from the 1970s. Peale explains how a positive attitude significantly increases your chances of success, and how motivational psychology is now employed in most walks of life. Salesmen are taught to believe that the word 'no' simply means that a customer has not yet said 'yes'. Positive thinking is now considered to be a key ingredient of sporting success. Professional golfers, for example, visualise the flight of each shot before they hit it. In rugby, place-kickers imagine the ball going straight between the posts each and every time.

---

[5] Botha, B.J., *The Sunday Times*, 8 January 2012.

Research has shown that the brain performs best when you have confidence in your ability to solve problems. So back yourself, and believe that you can do it.

As Henry Ford famously quipped, "Whether you think you can or you can't – you're right." So, visualise your success in the FAE examination. Keep this picture in your head at all times and it will help you to stay focused and meet your targets.

Perseverance

> "Genius is one per cent inspiration and ninety-nine per cent perspiration. Accordingly a genius is often merely a talented person who has done all of his or her homework."
>
> Thomas Edison

Perseverance and commitment are essential if you are to be successful in the FAE. You must recognise, however, that almost everything in life is habit forming. Your brain will perform at its best when its problem-solving capabilities are regularly challenged. Remember that it's more productive to study consistently on most days than to 'cram' for many hours every once in a while. This is particularly true of the FAE, where the case study technique is best acquired over time rather than by short periods of cramming.

The nineteenth century politician and writer, Benjamin Disraeli, emphasised the importance of perseverance when he said, "The secret of success is constancy of purpose."

So, commit yourself to the FAE. **Develop a regular study pattern**. Be patient as you learn the skills of problem solving across the range of FAE business disciplines. Most of all – **persevere!**

Summary

Most of us take the time to give regular checks to our cars and other possessions. Typically, however, we devote scant attention to the needs of our brain, despite the fact that, during our waking hours, we rely on it completely. This chapter has focused on the ways that the capacity of our brain can be optimised for the purpose of problem solving in the FAE.

Concentration is a key area of focus. Here, you must eliminate interruptions, get adequate relaxation, sleep well, eat healthily and take frequent study breaks. It is important too that you attempt case studies. This makes FAE problems more routine, so allowing your brain to provide solutions in a way that is faster and more reliable.

Positive thinking is another key component of problem solving. Always visualise your success in the FAE, keeping this picture in your head at all times. Finally, persevere and commit yourself to achieving that success.

---

[6] Peale, N.V (1974), *op cit.* n.3.

PART III

Problem Solving:
The Planning Stage

Chapter 4. Defining the Problem

Problem solving in the FAE requires, in the first instance, that you **correctly identify the problem** that needs to be addressed. At all costs you want to avoid investing valuable time trying to resolve the wrong problem.

Consider the dilemma faced by the owners of a large high-rise apartment building where most of the tenants were staying only a short time before moving out. The building was ideally located, being close to shopping facilities and transport connections. The neighbourhood was also highly regarded from a security perspective. Yet, despite its obvious advantages, in recent months there had been a mass exodus of tenants.

The owners hired a consultancy group to investigate the matter. Having interviewed residents and former residents the consultants presented their findings. The problem, they said, was that "… the apartment lifts were too slow". The owners examined options involving the repair of the old lifts. Unfortunately this would not resolve the issue, so the installation of new lifts was also considered. While this would provide an effective solution, the cost was prohibitively high.

Resigned to the continuing loss of tenants, the owners decided to sell the building. Before they did so, however, they were approached by one tenant who suggested an alternative solution. The problem was not the speed of the lifts, she said, but the fact that tenants got bored waiting for them. She suggested that TV monitors should be installed in the lifts, which would provide up-to-date news stories and sports results. Piped music in the lobby areas might also help, as would some tasteful paintings and sculptures to engage the interest of tenants waiting for the lifts to arrive.

Her proposal worked and the exodus of tenants stopped, allowing the owners to abandon their plans to sell the building. This story underlines the importance of accurately defining a problem so that efforts to find a solution are focused in the right direction.

Defining Problems in the FAE

The typical FAE case study involves a business entity that has a number of issues. These issues are called **primary indicators**. To correctly identify the indicators, you will need to proceed as follows:

1. What is Your Role?

Your role will largely determine the issues that you will need to address. For example, the marketing director in a business will be concerned with increasing sales revenue. The production director's responsibility is to ensure that finished goods are available on schedule and within budget. The CEO, however, will be anxious to ensure that all parts of the business are integrated optimally.

Thus, **defining your role is always the first step in an FAE case**. Consider Dublin City Rovers Football Club in **Supplement A** at the back of this book. Now I want you to study the first page of this FAE case and identify your role.

In the first paragraph of the case, you are introduced to Mary Thompson, a Chartered Accountant, who has recently been appointed as financial controller with Dublin City Rovers. Your role in this case is to complete the tasks assigned to Mary Thompson.

2. Identifying Indicators

Having established your role, it is now time to **identify the business issues** you will need to address – the primary indicators.

(a) Directed/Explicit Indicators Unlike the traditional style of other examination papers, an FAE case does not separately specify the requirements that the Examiner wishes you to address. Instead, you must become an **active participant** in the process. For example, this may involve attending a meeting with a client in your identified role. Following this meeting you should be in a position to determine what issues you will need to address. These may include issues that the client has expressed concern about, as well as others that, based on your professional judgement, will also need to be considered.

Directed indicators are those that are clearly signalled by the examiner. They will become evident from careful study of each FAE case. Directed indicators are commonly found in conversations between people in the case and in the minutes of meetings.

Directed indicators will be included in the main body of the case. An FAE Core Paper 1 case requires that approximately eight to ten indicators be specified.

EXAMPLE 4.1: IDENTIFYING DIRECTED PRIMARY INDICATORS

Referring again to Supplement A, the case of Dublin City Rovers, see if you can identify the **directed** indicators.

Solution

Mary has had a meeting with Bill Chester, the CEO of Dublin City Rovers. During this meeting, Bill has outlined the issues that need to be addressed.

- **Directed Indicator 1** At the end of the section on the Aviva Stadium, it states that "I have set out all the details of the Aviva Stadium arrangement in this document ... I would appreciate it if you could review the file and advise on the appropriate accounting treatment for this deal". This document is provided to you as **Appendix I**.
- **Directed Indicator 2** In the section entitled 'Opportunity – Aviva Stadium Tours', it states that "Now that we have settled into the Aviva ... we have a decision to make regarding the use of the stadium, in conjunction with the FAI and the IRFU, to offer stadium tours". Bill says later: "I said I would take

some advice and consider the two options – (a) a joint venture; or (b) going it alone – using strategic decision-making criteria". And further on he asks: "Will you analyse this based on suitability, acceptability and feasibility criteria?".

■ **Directed Indicator 3** In the section entitled 'Risk Register', it states that "I have taken the time to highlight some of the risks I see facing DCR" and you are provided with **Appendix II**. Mary assures Bill that she will review his risk list and prepare a note for the board, reminding them of their responsibilities, and incorporating the risks outlined by Bill.

■ **Directed Indicator 4** Under 'New Signing', the details of the signing of Zambian footballer, Mbuntu, are given and the various payments and dates involved in the deal. The final paragraph states: "Mary, as of yet no entry has been made in the financial records of DCR in respect of the above. I know Mbuntu will be a real asset to DCR on the football field. However, how can we recognise his value on our balance sheet? Please explain how we account for all of these payments. Make sure to include the relevant journal entries where appropriate".

■ **Directed Indicator 5** Under 'Agent's Fee', it states that "Jack observed that Mbuntu's agent, Fleecie … is demanding that his fee of €/£ 500, 000 is paid in bitcoin … What will we do?". You are told that "Mary reassures Bill that she can draft a note explaining what bitcoin is and why Fleecie might want to deal in it, as well as how the fee can be paid in bitcoin and at the same time mitigate any risks to DCR".

■ **Directed Indicator 6** Under 'Negotiation', it states that Bill "wishes to discuss a merchandising contract that has come up for renewal … Both companies [i.e. O'Neill's and Kappa] are competing for our business. Here are the details of their offers [see **Appendix III**]. What I would like you to do is review the offers and detail for me how we can close-out the negotiations to our advantage."

■ **Directed Indicator 7** Under 'Customer Insights', you are told that Bill hands Mary a sheet of paper (provided as **Appendix IV**), asking her "Mary can you help me understand the value of this data? And what steps are involved in a data exercise anyway? I'd appreciate any comments and insights you might have".

■ **Directed Indicator 8** Under 'Corporate Social Responsibility', Bill says "Mary, I would like you to give some thought to the Corporate Social Responsibility (CSR) section of our upcoming annual report", to which we are informed that "Mary immediately jumps at the chance to shape this section of the report. She commits to giving Bill an overview of the importance of CSR, and will also suggest a number of projects that she feels might complement Jack's altruistic intentions".

(b) Implicit Indicators These are issues that the examiner does **not explicitly request** in an FAE case. While not every case will have implicit indicators, it is important to be able to recognise the 'flags' when they arise. For example, a client may outline a number of areas of their business that they want advice on. A key feature of adding value to a client, however, is in identifying additional issues that need to be addressed. Implicit indicators often emerge from an integration of the directed indicators and other information provided in the case.

For example, a client may be considering the importation of components from a supplier located in a low-cost economy. These components are currently manufactured in-house. Your analysis of the case identifies the following directed indicators:
- computation of the cost of out-sourced components;
- the impact of out-sourcing on company morale;
- the cost of staff redundancies;
- ensuring that the quality of out-sourced components is satisfactory;
- alternative uses for the spare capacity created by the outsourcing of supplies;
- financial reporting implications of closing the manufacturing division;
- taxation implications of closing the manufacturing division;
- consideration of the strategic implications of outsourcing; and
- foreign exchange risk implications.

Further analysis and integration of the above issues may lead you to also identify the following **implicit** indicators:
- Risks arising from the remoteness of the supplier. These may include political, geographical and environmental risks. For example, many companies had supply-chain difficulties following the Japanese earthquake in 2011.
- There may be ethical issues relating to the working conditions and wage levels of the new supplier's staff. Such issues have often been controversial for companies that source their supplies from low-cost economies.

These are important considerations that are not immediately apparent from one's first reading of a case. Indeed, issues relating to risk and ethics are often significant but are not always signalled as direct indicators in a case.

Issues to avoid Knowing what issues **not** to address is an essential part of any assignment. You may perceive certain matters as being important, but a client may not want assistance with them. From an FAE perspective, it is critical to identify issues that the examiner wants you to steer clear of. Otherwise you may investigate an issue for up to 30 minutes before realising that it has been a complete waste of your time. However, you should exercise caution when a client suggests that some matter is irrelevant – using your professional knowledge you may decide that is not the case.

EXAMPLE 4.2: IDENTIFYING ISSUES TO AVOID

Brimeo Limited is currently considering the closure of its specialist wines' division. This division had been trading profitably for several years, but recently customers have been more interested in purchasing mid-range, less expensive wines. As marketing director of the company, you have been asked to make a presentation to the board outlining the key issues that should be considered in making this decision. A sub-committee, chaired by the HR director, has been appointed to examine the impact of the proposed closure on the company's workforce.

Comment

As marketing director of Brimeo Limited, you should focus primarily on the marketing implications of the proposed closure of the specialist wines' division. You may, of course, extend your analysis to identify strategic, taxation or other consequences of closing the division. You should **not**, however, examine the HR implications of the closure. These are being examined by a separate sub-committee and, as far as you are concerned, HR is **an issue to avoid**.

PRACTICE EXERCISE 4.1: IDENTIFYING ISSUES TO AVOID IN THE DUBLIN CITY ROVERS CASE

Have another look at the Dublin City Rovers case in **Supplement A**. See if you can spot any issues to avoid.

Summary

Before a problem can be solved it must first be properly defined. Often, large amounts of time are invested in trying to solve the wrong problem.

In FAE case studies you must first know what your role is before you can determine what issues need to be addressed. Essentially, your role is **who you are** and **what your job specification is** in the case.

The issues that you must address are called primary indicators. There are two types of primary indicator:
1. indicators that are clearly identified in the case – **directed** primary indicators; and
2. indicators that are not as clearly flagged – **implicit** primary indicators.

The majority of indicators in an FAE case are likely to be directed primary indicators. You should, however, be aware that some issues that are important may not be as clearly flagged by the examiner. Sometimes these can be identified by establishing linkages between the directed primary indicators. Issues relating to ethics, fraud, governance and risk may also be important.

Finally, there may be issues in the case that the examiner does **not** want you to address. These are **issues to avoid**, and you must be careful to identify them at an early stage so as not to waste valuable time.

The overall challenge of identifying the problems in each FAE case is outlined in **Figure 4.1**.

FIGURE 4.1: IDENTIFYING THE PROBLEM

Your Role (Identify)

Chapter 5. Linking the Case Information and the Primary Indicators

Imagine that you have purchased a flat-pack desk which must be assembled. You begin by scratching your head, wondering what problem-solving approach you will employ. You decide to organise the various parts that come in the box. So you group the four legs together, likewise the three drawers, and the top of the desk that will have come packed as one piece. Then you arrange the nuts, bolts and screws into little like-sized groupings. When you have everything organised, you are ready to start assembling. You begin to follow the steps in the instructions leaflet which, if you're like me, you will probably understand after the desk has been assembled!

A similar approach is used when assembling the information in an FAE case. As outlined in **Chapter 4**, you will have begun by identifying your role and making a list of the primary indicators. You are therefore aware of the principal issues/problems that must be addressed. The next step is to **organise the information** provided in the case. This requires that you read the case in detail from the beginning. As you read, it will help to form a picture of the scene being described.

You have three objectives:
1. to link the information in the case with the already-identified primary indicators;
2. to identify any additional indicators (implicit indicators), any issues to avoid, and any issues that you may have overlooked; and
3. to form the 'big picture' and so capture the key aspects of the case.

All three objectives are critical parts of the planning stage of the problem-solving process. The first two are addressed in this chapter, while the big picture is covered in **Chapter 6**.

Linking the Information with the Primary Indicators

The purpose of having delayed a detailed reading of the case now becomes clear. Having already identified the primary indicators, every line of the case can now be considered in the context of its use in addressing those indicators. This is a focused reading of the case. However, had you read the case in detail **before** identifying the primary indicators it would have had less value.

As you read, you should record the link between points or paragraphs in the case and one or more primary indicators. This information can be effectively catalogued by making a note in the margin. For example, if a line in the case relates to primary indicator 2, a note in the margin might read 'PI 2'. Case exhibits or appendices should be similarly classified, each being identified as relating to one or more specific primary indicators.

Let us consider the application of this technique with the help of a Practice Exercise.

> **PRACTICE EXERCISE 5.1: LINKING THE CASE INFORMATION AND THE PRIMARY INDICATORS**
>
> Revisit the Dublin City Rovers case in **Supplement A**. Re-read the case now from the beginning. Using the primary indicators as your reference point (see **Example 4.1**), underline or highlight relevant points in the case related to each primary indicator.

Additional Indicators and Issues to Avoid

A detailed reading of an FAE case gives you the opportunity to spot any additional indicators you may have overlooked previously, or any issues that you should avoid. It is **critical** to note the issues to avoid and to ignore them – don't invest time that will provide no return.

Summary

Organising the information in a case is a critical part of the problem-solving process. In the FAE this requires a detailed reading of each case study, which will enable you to link the information in the case to each issue/indicator that you need to address. You will also have the opportunity to spot any additional indicators that you may have previously overlooked and identify what issues to avoid.

The part that this plays in the overall problem-solving process is outlined in **Figure 5.1**.

FIGURE 5.1: LINKING INFORMATION TO THE PRIMARY INDICATORS

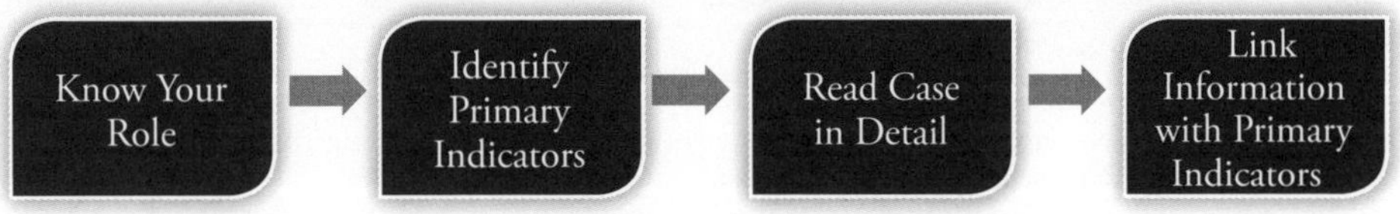

"Jenkins – shouldn't you be in assembly?"

Chapter 6. The 'Big Picture'

As a plane approaches its destination, have you noticed how, from a window seat, you can often see an entire city? By night, the contrast between its bright lights and the surrounding darkness marks the city's boundaries even more clearly. Upon landing, however, you are enveloped by a mass of sprawling buildings, and your sky view soon becomes a distant memory.

Have you ever watched a near accident unfold, as a pedestrian walks into the path of an oncoming car, forcing the driver to brake suddenly? Or perhaps, from some overhead vantage point, you have seen people wander about in a maze, searching endlessly for an exit.

Sometimes, having an overview of the issues allows us to find a solution for even the most difficult of problems. This insight, this overall perspective that empowers us to become expert problem solvers, is called the big picture. To become proficient at analysing and integrating information in the FAE, you must endeavour to see the 'big picture'.

FAE Case Studies and the Big Picture

What information is likely to make up the big picture in an FAE case? The answer to this question will vary, but certain core information is likely to feature in most cases:
- What type of business is it? Consider issues such as:
  - whether public or private;
  - the industry sector;
  - whether it is expanding or contracting;
  - its principal shareholders; and
  - its management structure.
- What are the indicators, i.e. what are the most critical issues facing the business?
- What links are there between the primary indicators?
- Are there any additional implicit primary indicators such as significant risks or important ethical issues?

These issues are outlined in **Figure 6.1**.

FIGURE 6.1: THE BIG PICTURE

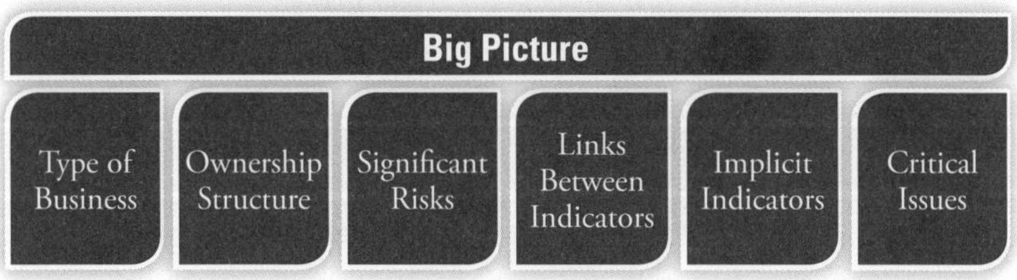

EXAMPLE 6.1: BIG PICTURE – DUBLIN CITY ROVERS

The big picture for Mary Thompson in the Dublin City Rovers case (**Supplement A**) is:

■ Dublin City Rovers (DCR) is a privately owned football club, which plays in the Championship of the English League.

■ DCR has recently moved to the Aviva Stadium, on a 10-year lease from the FAI and the IRFU, who are joint owners of the Aviva. The club was recently purchased by Jack Wa.

■ DCR is considering offering stadium tours, either as part of a joint venture with the FAI and the IRFU or on a stand-alone basis.

■ DCR has not kept its risk register up to date, and the board has not been proactive in identifying and planning for identifiable risks.

■ DCR is currently evaluating a major merchandising contract for its shirts, with two companies, O'Neill's and Kappa, having tendered offers for the contract.

■ DCR is planning a major initiative in the area of data analytics, particularly in relation to establishing the characteristics of its fan base.

An awareness of the big picture provides an overview insight into Dublin City Rovers Football Club. Like the view from a plane or from a perch overlooking a maze, the big picture allows us to capture the essence of the company, to identify the factors that are most critical to its future, and it also provides an understanding of how the key issues interact with one another.

Summary

Having a clear understanding of a problem is an essential part of the problem-solving process. An overview enables the problem solver to determine the issues that are most critical to a business. It also permits linkages to be established between the primary indicators that must be addressed in the case. This overview is called the big picture, and it is an integral part of the FAE problem-solving technique.

Chapter 7. The Planning Stage – Overview

Planning is a critical part of the problem-solving process. In every FAE case, planning should consist of four parts:
1. establish what your role is;
2. identify the issues that must be addressed (i.e. the primary indicators);
3. relate all information to the primary indicators; and
4. outline the big picture.

You have 30 minutes of reading time at the beginning of each FAE paper. You are not allowed to write in your answer book during that time, but planning should begin the first minute you have sight of the paper.

In the **Core Paper 1**, the planning stage, including the reading time, should take approximately 60–80 minutes. Having completed the planning stage, you will then have approximately 3 hours and 30 minutes to implement your plan.

For a four-hour case containing eight indicators, a useful rule of thumb is to spend five minutes planning each indicator, and 25 minutes writing your answer. This is in addition to the planning done during the 30 minutes of reading time.

The total time allowed for the end-of-year **Elective** exam (i.e. Paper 2) is also 4 hours, plus 30 minutes of reading time, but allocated between **two** cases. For this paper the best strategy is to use approximately 35 minutes for the planning stage of one of the two cases. This plan should then be implemented. The second case should then be attempted using a similar approach.

The planning stage of the problem-solving process is illustrated in **Figure 7.1**.

FIGURE 7.1: THE PLANNING STAGE OF THE PROBLEM-SOLVING PROCESS

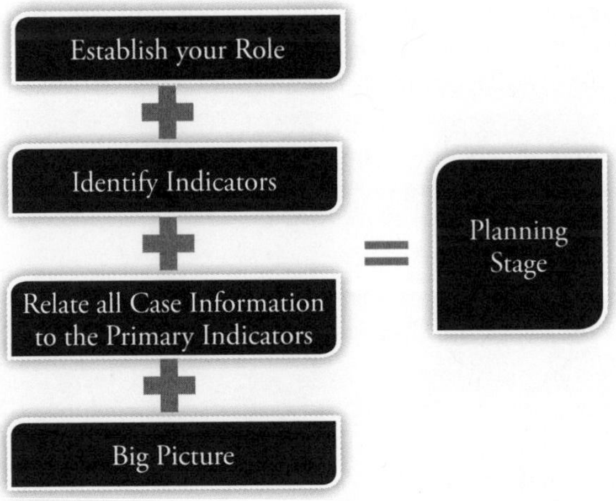

1. Establish what your Role is

The type of role that you play in an FAE case study can vary considerably. In one, you may be carrying out the duties of an external auditor or a financial consultant. In another, you might be the financial accountant in a public company or a private company's internal auditor. An FAE student must have a flexible mindset, one with the capacity to give attention to detail and the versatility to address issues across a range of business subjects.

Your first step in every FAE case study is to establish what your role is. This information will often be contained in the first page of a case. It will influence the way in which you analyse issues and the perspective from which you view them. For example, an internal auditor will be concerned with ensuring that a company's internal control system is effective in protecting its assets. The focus of an external auditor, however, is on being able to express an opinion on whether or not a company's financial statements give a true and fair view.

2. Identify the Issues that must be Addressed

Once you have determined your role, your next step is to identify what issues must be addressed. At this stage of the planning process you should **not** attempt a detailed reading of a case. Rather, you should only examine the case material to the extent that it is necessary to identify the issues that you must address.

In FAE case studies these issues are called primary indicators, and they can fall under two headings:

(a) Directed Indicators Directed indicators are issues that are clearly signalled in the case study. They are likely to arise from a request for information, a problem that must be resolved or some other reference to a matter that you must address.

(b) Implicit Indicators These are issues that are **not explicitly requested**, but which you nonetheless decide are important. Implicit indicators may relate to issues such as risk, security or ethics. They are likely to be far less numerous than directed indicators.

The Core Paper 1 case study will contain approximately eight to ten primary indicators, Each primary indicator will fall into one of the major subject areas identified in the FAE Competency Statement.

A case may also contain an instruction that certain issues should not be addressed. These are called **'issues to avoid'**, and it is imperative that you identify them so as to avoid wasting valuable time.

3. Link Information in the Case to the Primary Indicators

Once you have identified the primary indicators, you should read the case in detail. As you do so, you should consider how each sentence/paragraph can be used to address one or more primary indicators. You should also be on the lookout for additional primary indicators and issues to avoid.

4. Outline the 'Big Picture'

The 'big picture' is the final stage of the planning process. Here you create an overview of the key information in the case. It will contain important information about the business, any critical decisions it faces and any linkages between the primary indicators previously identified. The integration of information in the big picture may also enable you to identify an implicit indicator that you had not spotted previously.

Summary

The planning stage is a critical part of the problem-solving process. It begins when you have sight of the examination paper and consists of four parts:
1. establish what your role is;
2. identify the issues that must be addressed (i.e. the primary indicators);
3. relate case information to the primary indicators; and
4. outline the big picture.

It should be noted that only the material in your answer booklet will be marked by the examiner. Any additional sheets, etc., that are inserted in the answer booklet are destroyed prior to marking.

On completion of the planning stage, you will be well positioned to address the primary indicators in each case. The implementation of your plan comes next and is covered in detail in **Part IV**.

PART IV

Problem Solving:
The Implementation Stage

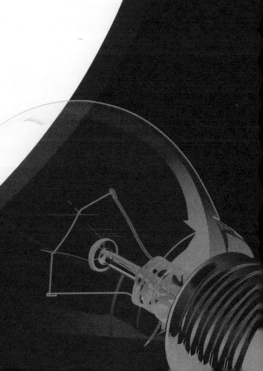

Chapter 8. Focus on Specifics

We have all listened to media interviews in which politicians and others engage in spin, skilfully avoiding questions posed by the interviewer. Such interviews are typically laced with general platitudes that are thought to appeal to a general audience.

An aspiring Chartered Accountant must possess a skill set precisely the opposite of that described above. In fact, the key skill demonstrated by a successful FAE student will be that of providing recommendations and solutions that are as **specific** as possible to the issue at hand.

Although the FAE is examined on an open-book basis, a candidate is almost certain to fare better by adopting a closed-book mindset. This involves using the specific information provided in a case, rather than relying on generic-style information that could be accessed in prescribed textbooks, course toolkits and other course materials. In fact, FAE candidates should generally have recourse to outside material only when all relevant information in the case has been used in providing one's answer.

In the exam, you may have access to study material that looks similar to what appears in an FAE case. You may even have a mock exam case that has covered similar ground. Remember, however, that you must address the specific circumstances of each case. Therefore, use the type of material described above with extreme caution.

The principle outlined above is clearly demonstrated in the Dublin City Rovers Football Club case in **Supplement A**. Let us consider it now.

EXAMPLE 8.1: FOCUS ON SPECIFICS – THE DUBLIN CITY ROVERS CASE

One of the primary indicators in this case is to review the club's risk register and to prepare a note for the board reminding them of their responsibilities in relation to dealing with the identifiable risks.

In addressing this indicator, it is essential to relate one's answer to the information provided in the case and the specific circumstances of the business.

You will recall that the club's CEO, Bill Chester, has identified some risks as he sees it. It would therefore be wise to focus on these risks, namely:

- demotion to the first division of the English Football League;
- revenue failure;
- lapsed insurance policies on players;
- managing the players' wages bill; and
- impact of Brexit on the club.

Analysis of Example 8.1

Example 8.1 demonstrates how to employ a focused approach to problem solving in the FAE. First, analyse the specific information provided in respect of a primary indicator. You should then consider additional information, specific to the circumstances and requirements of the business. In other words, one's answer should be relevant to a football club.

Example 8.1 also demonstrates the importance of having a detailed technical knowledge of the business disciplines that comprise the FAE. In this case, it will be necessary to be proficient in the area of risk assessment.

Read and Re-read the Primary Indicators

Each primary indicator (i.e. issue) is likely to comprise two or three lines. As you address a primary indicator, you should re-visit it frequently and read it afresh. Doing so may enable you to spot a nuance or direction that you did not notice previously. This will add depth to your answer. Re-reading a primary indicator will also make it more likely that you will stick to the point and provide information that is specific to the issue. The longer you continue to address an indicator without re-reading it, the more likely it is that your answer will become generic and less relevant.

Re-read the Parisian reference above – have you spotted the second 'the'?

Specialised Entities

It is quite common for an FAE case to be based on a specialist business or entity. While this may seem challenging, you should be reassured by the fact that you are not expected to have expert knowledge of such a business. Your answer must, however, reflect the specialist nature of the business. The key skill therefore is to apply general business principles to the particular circumstances of the business in question.

For example, a credit union will only lend to a customer when the lending officer believes that the loan will be repaid. As credit unions are 'not-for-profit' institutions, however, the lending criteria may be more accommodating of their members' needs. Also, as all loans are insured without any additional cost to the borrower, credit unions can be more flexible when a member is unable to service their loan commitments.

Thus, normal lending principles apply in relation to a specialised entity, such as a credit union. They are administered differently, however, as a credit union operates on a 'not-for-profit' basis. Similarly, a private hospital will have to balance the competing objectives of customer care and profitability. So, although normal commercial principles apply, they must be balanced with the need to ensure that patients are treated with dignity and respect.

Examiners use a broad range of businesses as a basis for examining students' knowledge of FAE material. Case studies have included an insurance brokerage, a crèche, a spirits manufacturer, a construction company and a company engaged in R&D for new technologies for smartphones and devices.

When dealing with a specialist entity in an FAE case, the challenge is to apply your business knowledge in a way that reflects the specific circumstances of the entity in question.

Summary

A focus on specifics is a prerequisite for success in the FAE. An entity's exact circumstances must be addressed when dealing with each primary indicator. A key skill, therefore, is the application of your professional knowledge in a way that is highly focused. The use of generic information is of limited value and, although the FAE is an open-book examination, it requires a closed-book mindset.

The same mindset extends to cases involving a **specialist** entity, such as a charity, a credit union or a private hospital. While general business principles are relevant, they must be applied in a way that fully reflects the particular objectives and circumstances of this type of entity.

When addressing a primary indicator, you should revisit the information provided in the case study several times during your planning and writing stages. This will ensure you understand it fully and will enable you to stay focused and direct when providing your answer. A good rule of thumb is to check that each paragraph you write references the case study, client or situation. If it does not you are in danger of providing a generic answer.

Chapter 9. Knowledge and the Three Dimensions

In every FAE case, 15–25% of the available marks relate to professional competency. The criteria on which this is evaluated are set out in **Appendix 2.3** of **Chapter 2**.

A student's ability to demonstrate professional competency will be enhanced by applying knowledge in three dimensions. This requires the exercise of the following skills:
- fundamental skills;
- value-adding skills; and
- advisory skills.

Fundamental Skills

These are the core skills that every Chartered Accountant is expected to demonstrate. They include the ability to identify and describe problems, and to effect calculations involving areas such as tax computations, variance analysis and the preparation of financial statements.

Value-adding Skills

Having executed the core skills (e.g. preparation of a draft tax computation before a client's year end), a Chartered Accountant should then meet with a client to explore further issues arising. For example, the purchase of equipment before the financial year end could optimise the use of capital allowances. The discussion could also include pensions and retirement planning and relevant capital acquisitions tax issues.

By assisting a client in this way, a Chartered Accountant is adding value, having already demonstrated the core skill of preparing the client's draft tax computation.

See **Chapter 11** for a further discussion of value-adding skills.

Advisory Skills

These are high-level skills that require a Chartered Accountant to exercise his/her professional judgement. They involve providing a client with conclusions, recommendations and advice based on the alternatives identified at the value-adding stage. For example, one might recommend to a client which of the foreign exchange risk management options would be most appropriate to his/her circumstances.

See **Chapter 12** for a further discussion of advisory skills.

The relationship between the three dimensions of knowledge is outlined in **Figure 9.1**.

FIGURE **9.1:** THREE DIMENSIONS OF KNOWLEDGE

Skills required of a Chartered Accountant	How Skill is Exercised
Fundamental	■ Identify ■ Describe ■ Explain ■ Calculate
Value-adding	■ Assess ■ Analyse ■ Expand ■ Compare ■ Integrate ■ Interpret ■ Outline alternatives ■ Identify need for additional information
Advisory	■ Outline implications of ■ Advise ■ Conclude ■ Recommend

The application of knowledge as outlined in **Figure 9.1** above, will greatly enhance one's ability to achieve a high score for professional competence in FAE cases.

Summary

An FAE candidate is expected to develop a skillset capable of applying business knowledge on three dimensions:
■ fundamental skills;
■ value-adding skills; and
■ advisory skills.

The appropriate combination of these skills will significantly enhance one's ability to demonstrate competence in the FAE.

Chapter 10. Exhibits and Calculations

Calculations are central to most of what a Chartered Accountant does. Whether computing a company's profit and tax liability, details of variances, the net present value (NPV) of a project or the cost of a product, an accountant is constantly working with numbers. Computations are time-consuming, however, and one can easily be led astray.

The key point is that **before** you do a computation you must know where it will take you. Do nothing unless you know precisely what a calculation will be used for. It is essential to realise that computations are just a means to an end. For example, a project's NPV will be critical in deciding whether it should be undertaken. An unfavourable sales price variance will require a review of a firm's pricing policy or perhaps a re-appraisal of its budgeted selling prices. A firm's weighted average cost of capital (WACC) provides the hurdle rate used to evaluate capital projects that, for a particular firm, are typical in terms of its risk profile.

'Use it or lose it' is a phrase commonly associated with rugby. It signals a warning from the referee that the team in possession must use the ball or he will award a scrum to the opposing team. 'Use it or lose it' also applies in the FAE. Having spent time doing a calculation, you **must use** the work that you have done, or the benefit will be lost. For example, based on an analysis of cash flows, you may conclude that a company should upgrade its IT system. You must communicate that conclusion to whomever you are reporting. In doing so, you should supplement your advice with relevant qualitative points.

You may advise, for example, that the new IT system should initially run in parallel with the old system. You will also stress the importance of data security during the changeover process. Therefore, used appropriately, calculations are a means to an end. What matters most, however, is that you use those computations to deliver a professional service that will add value to your client.

Using Exhibits

FAE cases typically contain one or more exhibits. Exhibits might include information such as a set of financial statements, a copy of board minutes, details of product costings or project cash flows, a list of variances, or a summary of a firm's accounting policies. Each exhibit should be evaluated in the context of how it can be used to address one or more of the primary indicators. This linkage must be established **before** you commence any time-consuming computational work. The steps are outlined sequentially in **Figure 10.1**.

FIGURE 10.1: USING EXHIBITS AND CALCULATIONS

FIGURE 10.1: USING EXHIBITS AND CALCULATIONS

When examining exhibits, you should be vigilant for any items that are significant or unusual. These may include:

■ high value items;
■ items involving a material change between periods;
■ amounts for which additional details or explanations are provided;
■ items that could be significant for legal or ethical reasons;
■ anything that could affect a company's going concern status; and
■ items that could result in a qualified audit opinion.

PRACTICE EXERCISE 10.1: MERCHANDISING PROPOSALS

In the Dublin City Rovers case (**Supplement A**), one of the primary indicators was the evaluation of merchandising offers from two shirt manufacturers.

Study Appendix III of the case and outline how the information can be used in deciding which of the offers Dublin City Rovers should accept.

Linking Calculations and Primary Indicators

The nature of a primary indicator will usually determine the type of calculation that is required in an FAE case. **Figure 10.2** provides some examples of primary indicators and the calculations required to address them.

FIGURE 10.2: LINKING CALCULATIONS AND PRIMARY INDICATORS

Primary Indicator	Typical Calculation Required
Evaluating an investment opportunity	Net present value
Addressing a solvency problem	Forecast cash flow
Managing risk (interest rate/foreign exchange)	Alternative risk management strategies
Purchase/sale of a business	Share valuation
Addressing a group profitability issue	Divisional contribution analysis

Summary

The preparation of calculations is a fundamental skill of a Chartered Accountant. It is an area in which an FAE student will be expected to demonstrate competency. However, calculations are time-consuming and in the FAE they should only be undertaken when it is clear that they are necessary in order to address a primary indicator. Calculations are a means to an end, and it is essential that one's results are used as the basis for a conclusion or recommendation. It is also important that one's findings are supported by appropriate qualitative analysis.

Chapter 11. Problem-solving Approaches

Introduction

A man was walking in a meadow when he happened upon a hole. Wanting to see how deep it was, he threw a pebble in the hole and waited for it to land. Hearing nothing, he picked up a larger stone and tossed it in the hole. Once again there was no sound. Scratching his head, he wondered what to do. Nearby, he found a medium-sized rock, and lifting it up he dropped it in the hole. He pricked up his ears and listened intently but heard nothing. Finding a huge boulder some distance away, he hauled it along the ground and levered it into the hole. He waited patiently, but once again he heard nothing.

The man sat on the ground exhausted. Suddenly, he saw a goat running towards him at full speed. He leapt aside and the goat flew past and jumped headlong into the hole. The man sat down again. Some time later, a farmer came walking up.
"Have you seen a goat?" he asked.
"No," replied the man, fearing that he might be blamed for the goat's disappearance down the hole.
"Well, he can't be gone far," said the farmer. "Sure, I had him tied to a massive rock."

To the man in this story the question of depth proved unfathomable. Had he sought to broaden his problem-solving approach he may have had more success. By persevering with larger stones, however, each time the problem grew bigger and the consequences (especially for the goat!) more serious.

Problem-solving Approaches

Imagine that a sudden gush of water comes through the ceiling as you sit on the couch watching television. You shriek with fright and, after gathering your thoughts, you sprint to shut off the water supply. The solution is as automatic as the problem, and it requires little thought or consideration.

Now imagine that you are sitting on the same couch, and you notice a drop land on the floor in the centre of the room. Your eyes are drawn upwards, and you stare intently as a drop gradually grows in size, its weight eventually causing it to lose its hold on the ceiling. You drift back to the television and laugh at something or other that appears on the screen. After a while your attention returns to the ceiling. A number of questions go around in your head:
- What has caused the leak?
- How can it be fixed?
- How much damage has it caused?
- What is the likelihood of other leaks elsewhere in the house?
- Should you submit an insurance claim to cover the cost of repairing the damage?

There are many issues to be addressed in the case of a 'drip-drip' leak. For example, the leak may have been caused by a broken roof tile, a burst pipe or an overflow from the water tank in your attic. The method of fixing the leak will depend largely on its cause, but there may, in any event, be a number of alternatives. To assess the damage, you will need to go upstairs and possibly also carry out an inspection of the attic. The question of locating other leaks will require a visual inspection throughout your house. Submitting an insurance claim will provide a cash inflow, but the cost of your premium will increase if you decide to forfeit your no-claims bonus.

The 'drip-drip' leak requires you to think in depth about the nature of the problem and how it can be solved. There are several variables to be considered, some of which are interlinked or interdependent. The solution to the 'drip-drip' leak requires the application of depth in the problem solver's thinking. In this way, it is more indicative of the challenges you will face in the FAE, than that provided by the sudden gush of water which points to an immediate, albeit temporary, solution.

Methods of Demonstrating Depth

Depth in the FAE can be demonstrated by gradually unwrapping the different layers of a problem. This requires that you organise your thought process in a logical, consistent, and yet creative manner. A variety of approaches can be employed, and they include the following:
1. a cradle-to-grave/chronological approach;
2. a conflicting perspectives approach; and
3. an establishing linkages approach.

1. Cradle-to-grave/Chronological Approach

A cradle-to-grave approach examines an issue from commencement to termination. A chronological approach traces the evolution of an issue over a period of time. Both approaches are broadly similar and they are considered together for the purpose of achieving depth in the FAE.

A primary indicator might, for example, require that you outline how an asset should be accounted for. Using a cradle-to-grave approach, you would proceed as follows:
■ at the time of purchase (consider recognition criteria, estimation of useful life, decommissioning costs and residual value);
■ during the asset's life (consider annual depreciation/amortisation, choice of cost or valuation model, accounting for revaluations and impairments, and revision of asset's useful life);
■ at the end of the asset's life (consider presenting as an asset held for sale, abandonment or disposal, and disclosure of profit or loss on sale).

It is critical, of course, that you only consider the above points to the extent that they relate to the specific asset in question. In respect of **land** for example, which normally has an infinite useful 'life', at the time of purchase it will only be necessary to consider recognition criteria. During the 'life' of the land, it will only be necessary to consider the choice of valuation model and how to account for revaluations and impairments.

PRACTICE EXERCISE 11.1: OUTSOURCING PROPOSAL

A company is considering outsourcing the manufacture of a component used in its production process. Outline what factors should be considered in making this decision.

---

2. Conflicting Perspectives Approach

Stakeholder theory maintains that business entities have a responsibility to other parties as well as to shareholders. Depth can be achieved by examining an issue from different perspectives, as long as those perspectives involve parties that can justifiably be regarded as stakeholders of the business.

PRACTICE EXERCISE 11.2: PROPOSED TAKEOVER

Rhyme Limited is currently the subject of a takeover bid. The chief executive, who stands to benefit substantially, is in favour of accepting the offer. The current year's financial statements are due to be announced shortly and the chief executive wants the profit figure to be as high as possible, with a view to ensuring that the bidder completes the deal. He has proposed minimising accruals and opting for accounting policies that will maximise profit.

In your capacity as the finance director of Rhyme Limited you have been asked to advise the board.

---

3. Establishing Linkages Approach

When a detective arrives at a crime scene, the first step is to gather evidence. In the following weeks witnesses will be interviewed to try and identify a suspect. The detective will then seek to establish links between the suspect and the crime using techniques such as DNA testing, fingerprinting, CCTV images and phone records. If any of these help the case, the detective will prepare a 'book of evidence' that will be used when the case comes to trial.

In a similar way, a doctor will examine the links between a patient's symptoms and the anatomy of an illness. An athlete will study food supplements and training methods to optimise his/her performance. Social networking sites routinely seek to establish links between users as a way of growing their businesses.

Likewise, establishing links is important if you want to achieve depth in the FAE. Business issues are often related and you should always be on the lookout for an opportunity to link the issues in a case.

PRACTICE EXERCISE 11.3: ESTABLISHING LINKS

Morse Limited is a manufacturer of fireplaces. The company, which is family-owned, has a long-established tradition of appointing its board members from the ranks of its skilled craftsmen.

"It's a way of ensuring that quality comes first," says Frank Morse, the company's major shareholder. Over the last two years, Morse Limited has seen its share of the fireplace market decline as other suppliers compete with cheaper but inferior quality alternatives.

You have been asked to advise the board as to what course of action it should pursue in order to arrest the company's decline.

Summary

This chapter has focused on the ways in which you can demonstrate depth in the FAE. The key requirement is that you organise your thinking in a way that is logical and consistent, but at the same time develop your capacity to think creatively. Depth, therefore, requires an approach that is more subtle and varied than merely increasing the size of stone that you drop down a hole.

Three approaches are outlined as examples of ways in which depth can be achieved:
1. the cradle-to-grave/chronological approach;
2. the conflicting perspectives approach; and
3. the establishing linkages approach.

These approaches are not intended to be exhaustive in terms of the methods you can employ to resolve problems; nor are they mutually exclusive. You can, for example, establish linkages between issues while also exploring them on a cradle-to-grave basis. What is important is that you integrate your knowledge in a way that is comprehensive, creative and consistent.

It is important to point out that depth does not equal length. Rather than writing at length on a particular point, you are more likely to demonstrate depth by making several points and employing a technique such as 'cradle-to-grave' to develop an issue.

Chapter 12. Be Decisive!

> "Have you always found it difficult to make decisions?" asked the doctor.
> "Well, yes and no", replied the patient, finding it hard to make up his mind.

Unfortunately, sitting on the fence is a luxury that an FAE student cannot afford. In a typical FAE case you will be required to make several decisions. For example:

- the possible closure of a division;
- whether to acquire a target company;
- whether a capital investment opportunity should be undertaken; and
- the optimal transfer price.

In addressing these questions, you may raise several more. Rudyard Kipling put it well in his poem, "The Elephant's Child":

> "I keep six honest serving-men
> (They taught me all I knew);
> Their names are What and Why and When
> And How and Where and Who."

Questions such as these may help you to comprehensively examine a primary indicator. You might identify a number of alternative courses of action, each with advantages that would cause you to favour it. Having considered all the alternatives, however, you **must ultimately choose only one.**

Your choice may depend on several factors. Maybe one investment opportunity has a higher NPV than another, or perhaps it has significant qualitative advantages that compensate for having a lower NPV. Maybe it is the best strategic fit for the company's overall operations, or perhaps it involves a lower level of risk than other higher NPV projects.

Regardless of the basis for your conclusion, it is critical that you provide a recommendation to whoever has requested your advice. In business, most information is prepared for decision-making purposes; this is certainly the case in the FAE. You may be reporting to your audit partner, to the client's chief executive or to its board of directors. Each will expect you to provide the information and the advice required for whatever decision they must take.

A key aspect of delivering a professional service is that the advice you provide is consistent with the underlying facts. Thus, it is critical in the FAE that your analysis is consistent with your computations, and that your advice is consistent with your analysis. This is illustrated in **Figure 12.1**.

FIGURE 12.1: DELIVERING A PROFESSIONAL SERVICE

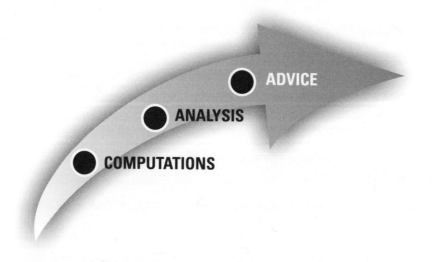

PRACTICE EXERCISE 12.1: ACCOUNTING POLICY CHOICE

Jupiter Limited has just acquired its first investment property for €4.2 million. You have been asked, in your role as an audit senior in Light, Torch, Byrne & Co., to outline what accounting treatment the company can adopt in respect of the newly acquired investment property.

You are aware that Jupiter operates an incentive scheme, whereby management bonuses are based on the company's annual profit figure. Jupiter revalues its land and buildings assets, as permitted by IAS 16 *Property, Plant and Equipment*. The finance director has expressed concern, however, regarding any unfavourable tax consequences of carrying investment property at a revalued amount.

Summary

The provision of a professional service demands that advice must add value, in terms of providing a client with a specific recommendation, supported by rigorous analysis, and with all significant assumptions clearly stated. Ultimately, it is the client who will make the decision, but the role of the Chartered Accountant is to recommend the alternative that is most appropriate to a client's circumstances.

The same principle applies in the FAE, and you should always ensure that you complete your answer to each primary indicator with a clear recommendation or conclusion.

Chapter 13. Executive Summary

The news on TV or radio invariably opens with a summary of the headlines. On their front page, newspapers flag the biggest stories of the day. Books do it on the back page, drawing you in by revealing an appealing outline of the plot. Websites, which rely on visitors to generate advertising income, operate in a similar way by flagging provocative headlines in an effort to grab our attention. Corporate annual reports provide yet another example, disclosing a five-year summary of key figures such as EPS and revenue in their opening pages.

Dining on the headlines has become the way of the modern world. In our busy lives we gravitate towards the bottom line, hoping to learn enough so that we appear to be well informed. Aware that the devil is in the detail, we decide to live a heavenly existence as we go about our hectic schedules.

The world of business is no different. Executives, not wanting to be swamped in detail, expect you to be brief. "How much will it cost? What's the bottom line?" they ask impatiently, demanding a one-line response. In business reports, the reader's eye is drawn to what has become known as the **executive summary**. Mulling over the findings and recommendations, they will open the main report only if they want to know more.

Consider the story of the family who arrive in London having lived in a rural area for many years. They go shopping in Harrods, and the youngest son asks his father if he will take him to see the toy section. His father takes the boy's hand, and as they walk along they see two metal doors in the middle of a long wall.
"What's that?" asks the little boy.
His father shakes his head and, as they watch, the doors open and an elderly lady steps inside. Their gaze remains fixed on the doors, and a minute later they re-open and a beautiful young lady steps out.
"Get your mother, son," says the man.

Now imagine that you are stepping into a lift on the 20th floor of a building. Your audit partner is standing alongside and you have 30 seconds to brief him/her on the main issues to be discussed with a client. The lift begins to descend and, drawing a breath, you begin what is known as the 'elevator pitch'.

In the FAE, an executive summary takes on the role of an elevator pitch and, like the lift in Harrods, it has the potential to change the appearance of your script. Admittedly, the examining team will read everything that you write, but an executive summary provides a focal point, allowing you to showcase your key findings and recommendations. For a modest investment of time, you can transform your script into a business report that will add value for your client, and provide something that your client will be happy to pay for.

If the action required of you in the case study would benefit from an executive summary, you should leave space at the beginning for its inclusion. It should contain a synopsis of the main issues you have addressed along with your key findings and recommendations. It is best to complete the executive summary as you go, taking a moment to add to it as you complete each primary indicator. In total, an executive summary should be no longer than a page but, by emphasising your professionalism, it will punch beyond its length and prove a useful ally in your quest to display competence. Note, however, that the executive summary should always be proportionate to the length of the case or solution.

See the sample executive summary in **Supplement B**.

Summary

An executive summary has the potential to transform your answer into a professionally prepared report. Include an executive summary at the front of each FAE case, outlining the principal issues you have addressed and your key findings. An executive summary should be no longer than a page and should be relevant and proportionate to the type of case you are working on.

Chapter 14. The Implementation Stage – Overview

Having completed the planning stage of the problem-solving process, you are ready to write your answer in each FAE case study. This is the point at which the work you have already done will begin to pay dividends. The implementation stage of the problem-solving process is outlined in **Figure 14.1**.

FIGURE 14.1: THE IMPLEMENTATION STAGE

1. Focus on Specifics

The exact circumstances of a business must be addressed when dealing with each primary indicator. The use of generic information is of limited value, and although the FAE is an open-book examination, it requires a closed-book mindset.

When addressing a primary indicator, you should re-visit it frequently, to ensure that you understand it fully, and to stay focused and direct in your answer.

2. Problem-solving Approaches

To demonstrate depth in problem solving, you must organise your thinking in a way that is logical and consistent. You must also be able to think creatively. Three approaches to achieving depth were outlined in **Chapter 11**:
1. the cradle-to-grave/chronological approach;
2. the conflicting perspectives approach; and
3. the establishing linkages approach.

These approaches are neither exhaustive nor mutually exclusive in terms of the methods that you can employ to demonstrate depth in problem solving. What is important is that you integrate your knowledge in a way that is comprehensive, creative and consistent.

It is important to point out that depth does not equal length. Rather than writing at length on a particular point, you are more likely to demonstrate depth by making several points, and by employing a technique such as the cradle-to-grave approach to develop an issue.

3. Be Decisive!

A Chartered Accountant does not have the luxury of being able to sit on the fence and outline many alternative courses of action. The provision of a professional service demands that advice must add value in terms of providing a client with a specific recommendation, supported by rigorous analysis and with all significant assumptions clearly stated. Ultimately it is the client who will make the decision, but the role of the Chartered Accountant is to recommend the alternative that is most appropriate to a client's circumstances.

The same principle applies in the FAE, and you should always ensure that you complete your answer to each primary indicator with a clear recommendation or conclusion.

4. Using Exhibits and Calculations

Calculations can be time consuming and time is a scarce commodity in all of the FAE papers. So before you embark on any lengthy computation, you must know precisely where it will lead you. If you are not sure how a calculation will be used to address a primary indicator – don't do it!

Once you complete an essential computation, don't abandon it and move on to something else, even if you are under time pressure. Always use the result as the basis for a recommendation, advice or a conclusion.

5. Executive Summary

An executive summary provides you with a focal point, allowing you to showcase your key findings and recommendations. An executive summary should appear at the front of each FAE case that you complete, and should summarise your key findings and recommendations. It should be no longer than a page, and it should summarise your key findings and recommendations.

Summary

Having completed the planning stage, you are ready to write your answer to each FAE case. This involves the implementation of your plan and it consists of the following steps:
■ focusing on specifics;
■ achieving depth;
■ being decisive;
■ using exhibits and calculations to address primary indicators; and
■ preparing an executive summary where relevant.

PART V

Business
Developments

Chapter 15. Keeping Up To Date

Every professional should be fully informed about their chosen area of expertise. A client's needs can extend across a broad range of business areas, and a Chartered Accountant should be up to date with global and domestic economic developments. An awareness of current events and their implications can also assist in demonstrating competence in the FAE. While the cases require a candidate to focus on the circumstances of a particular business, every entity operates against the backdrop of broader economic events and an awareness of these can inform and enhance the advice that you provide to a client.

You should, therefore, keep up to date with major developments in the business world. Reading the business pages on a daily basis is a useful habit, with the *Financial Times* being a particularly good source of information. **Figure 15.1** demonstrates how you can track economic events and analyse their potential implications for business.

FIGURE 15.1: POSSIBLE IMPLICATIONS OF SOME NATIONAL AND INTERNATIONAL EVENTS

Event	Possible Implications
Brexit	Increased costs of exporting to/from the UK
	Increased volatility in the Sterling to euro exchange rate
	Issues relating to staff mobility
Security breaches	Increased focus on data security and prevention of viruses, ransomware, and other IT threats
Terrorism	Increase in global security measures to prevent terrorist attacks
Rise of right-wing populism	Less international co-operation between countries
	Increased tariffs on goods and services being exported
Increased competition for investment	Lower tax rates
	Less permanency in employment contracts
Natural disasters, e.g. the Japanese earthquake in 2011	Companies review policy of locating supply chain on a remote basis in cheaper economies
Rationalisation of financial services sector	Less competition between banks and, thus, higher borrowing costs for business

Event	Possible Implications
Scarcity of funding	Capital rationing becomes a more relevant factor and, therefore, increased focus on NPV
Falling property prices	Negative equity for businesses holding property assets
	Impairment losses in income statement
	Property less valuable as collateral for borrowing purposes
Falling consumer spending	More pressure on businesses to compete on price and quality
Falling unemployment	More competition for scarce labour resources
	Upward pressure on wages and salary costs, with consequent negative impact on profits
Emerging technologies	A shift in the factors of production resulting from advances in artificial intelligence
	Automation of back-office functions, such as record-keeping and payroll
	Work practice changes with services being provided from remote locations
	Increased use of cryptocurrency, such as bitcoin and libra, to settle business transactions
	Increased security, immutability and transparency provided by blockchain

Summary

FAE candidates should keep up to date with economic developments and their implications for businesses. Enhancing your knowledge in this way can be useful in demonstrating depth in the FAE. It also represents a valuable lifelong investment in advancing your future career.

PART VI

Overall Summary

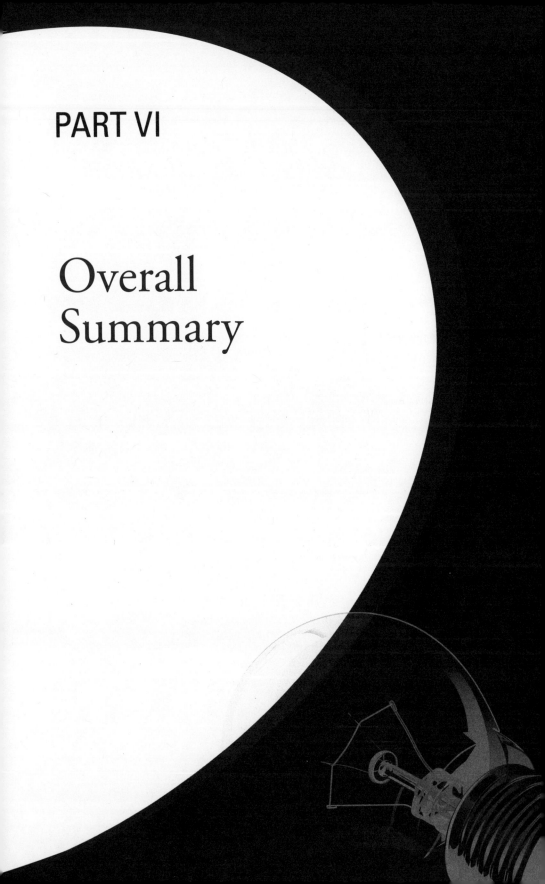

Chapter 16. Overall Summary

An FAE student must be willing to advise on matters of detail, as well as being knowledgeable on broader issues such as strategy. In fact, an FAE candidate is required to be proficient in numerous business disciplines. An FAE candidate is also expected to integrate material from these disciplines when addressing business issues.

The important issues that arise in FAE cases are called **primary indicators**. Addressing these issues and resolving them satisfactorily is an exercise in problem solving. The objective of this book is to provide FAE students with an effective problem-solving approach that will enable them to resolve issues and report in a way that demonstrates the professionalism expected of a Chartered Accountant.

For candidates to be successful in the FAE, they must satisfy two key prerequisites:
1. possess the required level of technical knowledge across the syllabus; and
2. apply that knowledge in a specific way to the circumstances presented in each FAE case.

Overview of the Problem-solving Approach

The problem-solving approach set out in this book is summarised under the following headings.

Know the Requirements

The **structure** and method of **assessment** of the FAE are outlined in **Part 1** of this book. You should ensure that you are fully conversant with these rules. To pass the FAE, you should ensure that you are fully conversant with these rules.

Lay the Foundations

"A focused brain always delivers power." This statement from **Chapter 3** emphasises the importance of maximising your brain power. This requires that you develop your capacity to concentrate; that you simulate exam conditions; that you think positively at all times; that you commit yourself to the FAE; and that you persevere with that commitment.

Problem Solving – the Planning Stage

You must begin by establishing what your **role** is in each FAE case. You should then identify the **primary indicators**. These can comprise directed primary indicators and implicit indicators. Issues to avoid, i.e. issues that must **not** be addressed, should also be identified.

You should then **read the case in detail** and establish how each piece of information, including exhibits, can be used to address the primary indicators. You should complete the planning stage of each case by creating the **big picture**, which should capture the key aspects of the business and the challenges facing it. The planning stage is summarised in **Figure 16.1**.

FIGURE 16.1: THE PLANNING STAGE OF THE PROBLEM-SOLVING PROCESS

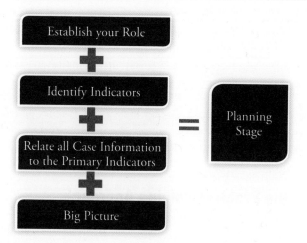

Having completed the planning stage, you are now ready to write your answer.

Problem Solving – the Implementation Stage

You must deal with the exact circumstances of a business when addressing each primary indicator. **Specific** points are required and offering generic information is of very little value.

You should only carry out time-consuming **calculations** if you are certain that your results can be used to address a primary indicator. Computations are usually based on one or more exhibits that are provided as part of an FAE case.

Fifteen to twenty-five per cent of the available marks in each FAE case study relate to professional competency. To demonstrate professional competency, you must organise your thinking in a way that is logical and consistent. Rather than writing a lengthy point, you should aim to develop an issue by making several succinct points. **Chapter 11** suggests three approaches to problem solving, which can be helpful in demonstrating professional competency: cradle-to-grave, taking conflicting perspectives, and establishing linkages.

You must be **decisive**. While it is important to consider all viable alternatives, you must ultimately decide which option is best. You must reach a conclusion, and include definitive advice in your report, taking care to note any key assumptions that underlie your recommendation.

Where appropriate you should attach an **executive summary** to the front of your case solution. This should be no more than a page in length and you can update it as you finish each primary indicator. The executive summary should identify the main issues faced by a business along with your key findings and recommendations.

The implementation stage is summarised in **Figure 16.2**.

FIGURE 16.2: THE IMPLEMENTATION STAGE

Chapter 17. Step-by-step Guide to an FAE Case Study

This chapter provides a focused synopsis of the approach set out in this book. It is intended as a reference point for students who have read and understood the ideas, suggestions and solutions that have been proposed throughout this book. This chapter summarises the two key areas of the problem-solving approach that has been proposed.

The Planning Stage This represents the time that you spend planning your answer to an FAE case study. In the examination it will include the reading time that you have at the beginning of each paper. This is likely to be supplemented by additional time that you allocate to the planning of your answer. During the planning stage, you will assimilate and integrate the case material so that you have a full understanding of the issues that must be addressed and how you should approach them. The planning stage is an integral and essential part of attempting each FAE case study.

The Implementation Stage Here you will be using your plan to address each of the issues in a case. Your answer should be written in a professional manner, employing reasoned arguments that relate to the specific information contained in the case. To display competence to the examiner, you will be expected to show proficiency in respect of fundamental skills, value-adding skills and advisory skills.

Based on the problem-solving approach outlined above, the following is an overall step-by-step guide to completing an FAE case study.

The Planning Stage

1. Establish what your role is (i.e. who are you in the case?).
2. Identify the primary indicators (and the issues to avoid).
3. Read the case in detail and relate all information to the primary indicators.
4. Draft the big picture.

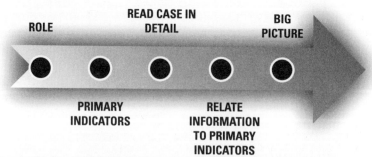

Having completed the planning stage, you are now ready to write your answer.

Implementation Stage

5. Address each primary indicator with points that are specific to the circumstances of the business.
6. Prepare calculations that are essential to address a primary indicator.
7. Achieve depth by the skilful development of your points. Use techniques such as a cradle-to-grave approach, a conflicting-perspectives approach or establishing linkages approach, and integrate the material in the case.
8. Be decisive! Reach a conclusion or make a recommendation, and ensure that this is included in your report.
9. Prepare a relevant executive summary.

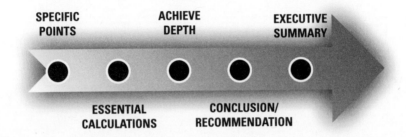

Supplements

Supplement A – FAE Core Paper 1*

Dublin City Rovers Football Club

(Suggested time 240 minutes)

Introduction and Background

Mary Thompson is three years post-qualified as a Chartered Accountant. After completing her training with a large accounting and auditing practice, Mary made the move into private industry working in various accountancy roles and broadening her experience until she felt ready for the next step. Today, July 1 2019, Mary has just been appointed to the role of financial controller of Dublin City Rovers Football Club (DCR). DCR has a year end of 30 June each year and prepares its accounts under IFRS.

As a former football player, Mary enjoyed a successful football career, playing for Arsenal and Ireland. Mary captained Ireland at the 2011 FIFA Women's World Cup where Ireland came third. An injury in the 2012/13 season saw an end to Mary's playing career; however, being interested in the financial side of the football business, Mary started on the road to becoming an accountant.

Mary's mix of experience as a professional player and her subsequent qualification as a Chartered Accountant meant that Jack Wa, new owner of DCR, had no hesitation in hiring Mary for this challenging role.

DCR was established in 1901 and is based in Dublin. Ten years ago DCR enjoyed the most successful year in its club history, winning the UEFA League Cup by beating Porto FC (Portuguese football club) on penalties after a lacklustre 120 minutes nil-all draw. At the invitation of the English FA, DCR decided to participate in the English football leagues and started a new life in the Championship. A few years previously there had been rumours of Wimbledon FC moving to Dublin that didn't work out, however the English FA saw DCR's success as a great football story and was keen to be associated with its whirlwind year, which captured the European footballing public's imagination.

DCR achieved mid-table success in the English Championship. However, the arrival of new owner, Jack Wa, at the end of the 2017/18 season saw an uplift in fortunes for the club. Jack owns the Goohui phone and communications company. Jack set up Goohui in Dublin in 2012, in the Silicon Docklands region of Dublin, and now employs 3,000 people. Jack, a billionaire and football fanatic, became an ardent supporter of DCR and it was inevitable that Jack would want to get further involved in this historic club.

DCR enjoyed unprecedented goodwill from the Irish public. However, DCR's original ground was too small, with a capacity of only 2,500 seats, so the ground quickly became untenable and DCR terminated its lease and vacated the ground in the 2014/15 season. The plan to build a state of the art stadium never materialised. Dubbed the 'Dublin City Ramblers' by media

---

* Sample paper based on 2019/2020 FAE Competency Statement.

and fans, until January 2019 DCR was renting out grounds all over the country for home matches on a one-off rental per match. For example, when DCR drew Manchester United in the third round of the FA Cup a few years' back, DCR cut a deal with the GAA (Gaelic Athletic Association) to rent its flagship stadium, Croke Park, for the home fixture; it was a complete sell out of 82,000 seats. By comparison, when DCR played Rotherham FC back in October 2018, Dalymount Park, with a capacity of 4,300, was rented. This unsatisfactory arrangement has tested relations with ardent fans who have stuck with DCR through thick and thin. DCR has also been dogged by unsympathetic journalists all too eager to use the lack of a permanent home as a stick to beat the club's management with.

Under Jack's investment in the club and, more recently, a permanent home ground, DCR's league position has climbed and this year saw it narrowly miss out on promotion to the Premier League, losing a play-off against Aston Villa FC.

This morning Mary is in DCR's headquarters, which is a floor in Jack's Goohui building; Mary is meeting with Bill Chester, the club's chief executive, to discuss a number of emerging issues and Mary's immediate priorities.

Bill, a lifelong football fan and chief executive of DCR for the past 10 years, greets Mary with a warm welcome and after some small talk recalling some of Mary's playing career highlights, an amiable Bill settles down to business. "Mary, this is such an exciting time for DCR. Since Jack decided to get involved the club has taken an enormous leap forward. Until now we have been using a group of advisors to provide accounting and support services. However, Jack has upped the profile and activities of the club in every way and we now need to build our own dedicated finance team."

The Aviva Stadium

Bill continues; "Our travails with a stadium have dogged us for the past number of years, prior to Jack coming on board. We thought we were clever matching what we thought would be demand for tickets with hiring stadia to meet that demand. We thought we were keeping the costs down. We utterly underestimated the goodwill and support from all over the world for DCR. Our actions meant we lost many revenue-earning opportunities as we were always oversubscribed for tickets. We were too cautious in not hiring out bigger stadia … and it was beginning to have an impact on the morale of the team.

"In January 2019 we struck a deal with the FAI (Football Association of Ireland) and the IRFU (Irish Rugby Football Union). They needed an anchor tenant to guarantee them a regular income, and as we are in the same business we have agreed flexibility where possible. There is good synchronisation between national and domestic football fixtures. There are potentially some clashes in March, with the Rugby Six Nations tournament where we potentially clash on three dates. However, both sporting codes and broadcasters have tremendous sway in re-arranging fixtures in a satisfactory manner. It is working out well and since we moved in average attendance over the last 10 home matches is 40,500. I have set out all the details of the Aviva Stadium arrangement in this document [see Appendix I]. We have not reflected the new arrangement in the year-end accounts so I would appreciate it if you could review the file and advise on the appropriate accounting treatment for this deal."

Opportunity – Aviva Stadium Tours

Mary learns that there is a board meeting in a couple of days' time where the board will try to decide on revenue-maximising strategies. "Now that we have settled into the Aviva," Bill continues, "we have a decision to make regarding the use of the stadium, in conjunction with the FAI and the IRFU, to offer stadium tours. The Aviva does have some experience of doing this, but it isn't something that either the FAI or IRFU have taken very seriously up until now. They depend on corporates hiring out suites to generate additional revenue. The IRFU season is short, and the FAI campaigns are drawn-out with long gaps between games. Consequently, they have struggled to build momentum in attracting visitors.

"Given the fact that we will have home matches every other week, the other two bodies are now keen to develop this stadium tour opportunity. Revenue and operating costs would be split three ways. The FAI and IRFU have a contact with a very experienced events management company, which would manage the running of tours. There is disagreement among our board, however. Half the board members feel that the FAI and IRFU are dependent on us to deliver the footfall, and believe that we should go it alone. These members point to the fact that, unlike domestic football, the playing season for rugby and international football is not consistent. They feel further justified in their view as the FAI and IRFU are prepared to shoulder the development costs to put a walkway and viewing point on the roof and other renovations to create a bespoke visitor centre. For our board meeting next week I said I would take some advice and consider the two options – (a) a joint venture; or (b) going it alone – using strategic decision-making criteria. I've since spoken with a peer in the GAA, which operates a similar model in-house at Croke Park. It receives 150,000 visitors per year; at an average gross revenue per head of €/£ 30. Operating costs associated with running it are €/£ 12 per head. The FAI and IRFU have quietly indicated that the expected operating cost will be around €/£ 6 per head, including the event company's fee. Will you analyse this based on suitability, acceptability and feasibility criteria? I intend to bring a recommendation to the board. Jack's view, for what it's worth, is that we should collaborate with our landlords. If we did decide to go it alone, it wouldn't be necessary to consider how the capital expenditure would be funded."

Mary agrees that she will do as Bill has asked based on the facts presented.

Risk Register

Bill changes the conversation now and smiles. "This will sound paradoxical, but you know that we were under enormous pressure over the past couple of years, and we neglected to keep the risk register up to date." Mary sympathises with Bill, but reminds him of the importance of such a document. Bill is pleased to hear Mary's comments recognising the risk register's importance and asks her to prepare a note to remind the board of its obligations in this regard. Bill continues, "I have taken the time to highlight some of the risks I see facing DCR" and passes a sheet of paper across the desk [see Appendix II].

Mary assures Bill that she will review his risk list, and that she will prepare a note for the board reminding them of their responsibilities that incorporates the risks he has identified.

New Signing

Bill changes subject now and wishes to talk about an exciting announcement that will be made in the coming days. Jack has persuaded the up-and-coming Zambian footballer, Mbuntu, to join DCR on a four-year deal. Mary is impressed, recalling Mbuntu's recent performances at the Africa Cup of Nations tournament, where he displayed great maturity and leadership for a 17-year-old midfielder. Bill quickly gets into specifics: "Jack was in Zambia on business and he found out that Mbuntu, whose parents and grandparents were educated by Irish missionaries, has a great affection for Ireland and always wanted to come to Ireland. On 1 April 2018, Jack met Mbuntu and his agent and they shook hands on a deal to play for DCR for a four-year period, subject to Mbuntu passing a medical.

"This medical was successfully completed on 30 June 2019. On the same date DCR paid €/£ 5,000 to Mbuntu's Zambian club, Zesco United, for the formal transfer of the player's registration rights to DCR. In addition, DCR have agreed to pay a €/£ 2 million signing-on fee to Zesco United as well as a €/£ 500,000 payment to Mbuntu's agent, Fleecie. Both of these amounts are expected to be paid in the coming weeks. It is also my understanding that Zesco United is now obliged to pay a fee of €/£ 100,000 to Mbuntu's childhood football club, Nchanga United, in relation to this subsequent sale of Mbuntu.

"The representatives of DCR and Mbuntu's agent have agreed that the player will be paid an annual salary of €/£ 1.5 million. An upfront signing-on bonus of €/£ 250,000 for the player was also agreed, subject to Mbuntu completing his four-year contract with DCR. This bonus was paid by DCR on 30 June 2019.

"Mary, as of yet no entry has been made in the financial records of DCR in respect of the above. I know Mbuntu will be a real asset to DCR on the football field. However, how can we recognise his value on our balance sheet? Please explain how we account for all of these payments. Make sure to include the relevant journal entries where appropriate." Mary nods enthusiastically as she is really excited at the prospect of this talented player coming to DCR.

Agent's Fee

Bill continues, "Jack observed that Mbuntu's agent, Fleecie, is a colourful character to say the least. He kept trying to change the terms of the deal. Mbuntu had to instruct him to leave the meeting at one point. Anyway, Fleecie is continuing his antics with an unusual request." Bill pauses, and Mary encourages him to continue. "Fleecie is demanding that his fee of €/£ 500,000 is paid in bitcoin. Now, I have checked and the currency of Zambia is not bitcoin, it is the Zambian kwacha, although US dollars are also widely accepted. I do recall hearing something about bitcoin, but I don't know what it is. What will we do?" asks Bill.

Mary reassures Bill that she can draft a note explaining what bitcoin is and why Fleecie might want to deal in it, as well as how the fee can be paid in bitcoin and at the same time mitigate any risks to DCR.

Negotiation

A relieved Bill thanks Mary and moves onto his next point. He wishes to discuss a merchandising contract that has come up for renewal. Bill continues the conversation: "This is one of the things that DCR as a brand has managed to get right. We sell a lot of jerseys, hats and scarves every year. We have always kept our manufacturing supplier local to us, so it was a good media story when the economy was in recession a few years back. Now though, we have outgrown the local supplier's capacity – last year we sold close to 25,000 shirts, which meant we had to order 5,000 shirts each from O'Neill's and Kappa. Both companies are competing for our business. Here are the details of their offers [see Appendix III].

What I would like you to do is review the offers and detail for me how we can close-out the negotiations to our advantage. This deal is just for the rights to supply the team and sell DCR shirts and other merchandise. To be clear, Jack will be putting the Goohui logo on the front of the shirts, considering he owns the club!"

Customer Insights

Bill thanks Mary for her willingness to address all the issues presented thus far, and says he has only one or two matters left. "Jack is very keen to understand our fan base. He was talking about fantastical software that he uses to analyse data to reveal insights. All very well I told him, but our systems are old and disparate; I don't believe he can get anything of any use from them. We did have to install barcode scanners a number of years ago, for when fans go through the turnstiles, to comply with FIFA directives that all matches are seated. The barcode scanners are mobile units, because we used grounds all over the country."

Mary enquires where this data from the turnstiles might be located. "One of Jack's guys took it off me last week; he said something about a data exercise, whatever that means. He claims to have fixed the data and sent me on a bunch of numbers and a couple of diagrams. I don't know if anyone has done anything with this information. We certainly have not discussed it at board level. You are welcome to look at them." Bill hands Mary a sheet of paper [see Appendix IV] and asks, "Mary, can you help me understand the value of this data? And what steps are involved in a data exercise anyway? I'd appreciate any comments and insights you might have." Mary nods enthusiastically and tells Bill she will have a look at it and give him some analysis.

Corporate Social Responsibility

Bill gratefully hands over the server box and remarks that he has one final issue to discuss. "Mary, I would like you to give some thought to the CSR section of our upcoming annual report. I know we are a while away from having the year-end accounts finalised. In the past we have traditionally paid lip service to this section of the report, with the inclusion of all sorts of inspirational pictures and content. Jack is keen to demonstrate his commitment to the club and would like to use this section of the report as a means of kick-starting any initiatives that we might like to include."

Mary immediately jumps at the chance to shape this section of the report. She commits to giving Bill an overview of the importance of CSR, and will also suggest a number of projects that she feels might complement Jack's altruistic intentions.

APPENDIX I – **MAIN PROVISIONS OF LONG-TERM LEASE OF AVIVA STADIUM**

DCR have agreed to lease the Aviva Stadium from the FAI and the IRFU for a period of ten years, commencing 1 January 2019. During this period, DCR will host all of its home football fixtures at the Aviva Stadium and will also be entitled to all ticket, hospitality and other revenues earned. However, DCR does not have the option to extend the lease or to purchase the Aviva Stadium outright.

DCR paid a non-refundable deposit of €/£ 300,000 on 1 January 2019, and has agreed to make an annual payment of €/£ 12,750,000 to the FAI and the IRFU on 31 December for each year of the lease period.

DCR has incurred, and paid, legal fees of €/£ 25,000 specific to this lease agreement. The Aviva Stadium has an expected useful life of 20 years. The interest rate implicit in the lease is 10% per annum.

Prior to the move to the Aviva Stadium, DCR leased Dalymount Park for the months of November and December 2018. Under the terms of the lease, DCR paid an amount of €/£ 15,000 to the owners of Dalymount Park on the final day of each month. Whenever possible, DCR adopts a policy of not capitalising leased assets.

APPENDIX II – **RISK REGISTER RISKS AS OUTLINED BY BILL**

- Demotion to the first division in the English Football League
- Revenue failure for DCR
- Letting insurance policies on DCR players lapse
- Managing the players' wages bill
- Impact of Brexit on DCR

APPENDIX III – DETAILS OF PROPOSED SHIRT AND MERCHANDISE DEALS

Replica Shirt and Merchandise Contracts (Proposed)		
	O'Neill's	**Kappa**
Origin of supplier	Ireland	Italy
Proposed contract length	3 years	5 years
Proposed fee for whole contract	€/£ 2.1m	€/£ 3m
Percentage royalty on volume sold each year	7.5%	5%
Official selling price per shirt	€/£ 70	€/£ 75

Notes:
1. O'Neill's fee is paid to DCR at €/£ 700,000 per year for each of the three years.
2. Kappa will pay €/£ 1 million in the first year of the contract, and €/£ 500,000 for each of the remaining four years of the contract.
3. Royalties receivable from O'Neill's are fixed at the volume quoted and guaranteed to be paid to DCR regardless of whether O'Neill's sell that indicated volume. However, DCR does not benefit incrementally if O'Neill's sell more than the indicated volume.
4. Kappa royalties are variable, in line with the volume sold. However Kappa are very confident about its market research into the potential market for DCR shirts, hence their willingness to pay a bigger fee in year one.

O'Neill's Market Research on Demand for DCR Shirts					
	2019/20	**2020/21**	**2021/22**	**2022/23**	**2023/24**
Forecast sales volume	50,000	50,000	50,000	–	–

Kappa Market Research on Demand for DCR Shirts					
	2019/20	**2020/21**	**2021/22**	**2022/23**	**2023/24**
Forecast sales volume	75,000	75,000	75,000	75,000	75,000

DCR Board Position

DCR wants to negotiate a contract for three years, earn a contract fee of €/£ 2.25 million and receive a royalty percentage of 8% based on selling 40,000 shirts per annum at €/£ 80 per shirt.

Bill disagrees with €/£ 80 per shirt as the market only commands €/£ 70–75, depending on how big the football team is. Bill has also found out that only the 'super clubs' in football command royalty premiums of 8%–10%.

DCR has a cost of borrowing/cost of capital of 9%.

Payments from O'Neill's and Kappa would be received annually in advance on the 1 July.

APPENDIX IV – TURNSTILE DATA*

League Home Games – 2017/18 Season

	19/08/17	02/09/17	16/09/17	30/09/17	14/10/17	28/10/17	11/11/17	25/11/17	09/12/17	23/12/17
League table position	9	11	13	12	14	10	11	11	11	13
Attendance	8,900	7,500	6,200	7,800	8,000	10,000	6,000	5,000	5,500	4,000

League Home Games 2017/18 Season (continued)

	06/01/18	20/01/18	03/02/18	17/02/18	03/03/18	17/03/18	31/03/18	14/04/18	28/04/18	12/05/18
League table position	15	14	16	17	18	18	18	17	17	16
Attendance	3,000	4,900	2,700	2,500	2,000	2,300	2,400	3,900	4,100	3,400

League Home Games 2018/19 Season

	18/08/18	01/09/18	15/09/18	29/09/18	13/10/18	27/10/18	10/11/18	24/11/18	08/12/18	22/12/18
League table position	10	11	11	12	10	10	8	9	7	7
Attendance	7,750	6,890	9,000	12,000	4,100	5,500	6,250	10,800	8,000	11,000

League Home Games 2018/19 Season (continued)

	05/01/19	19/01/19	02/02/19	16/02/19	02/03/19	16/03/19	30/03/19	13/04/19	27/04/19	11/05/19
League table position	7	9	10	7	6	6	5	5	5	5
Attendance	50,900	47,850	33,600	29,470	34,900	27,100	37,480	45,000	48,500	50,200

* Data prepared by Jack's employee.

APPENDIX IV – **TURNSTILE DATA (Continued)**

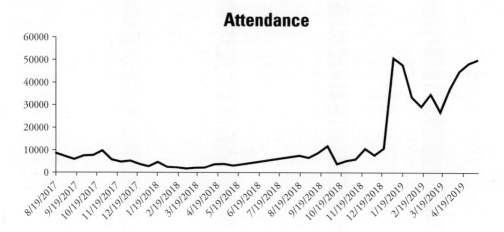

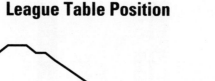

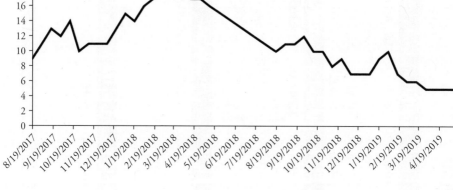

Supplement B – Sample Executive Summary

Dublin City Rovers Football Club

1. Lease of Aviva Stadium

The lease of the Aviva Stadium should be recorded as a non-current asset and as a liability in the financial statements of Dublin City Rovers Football Club (DCR).

2. Stadium Tours

Based on the willingness of DCR's partners to fund the capital element of the project, and the potential upside in return for minimal input, DCR should enter into a joint venture with the FAI and the IRFU.

3. Development of a Risk Management Strategy in DCR

The board of DCR is responsible for managing the company's identifiable risks. The stages of risk assessment and analysis are set out in this report. This reveals Brexit as being the risk that has the most strategic impact on DCR.

4. Signing of Mbuntu

The costs of signing Mbuntu should be recorded as an intangible asset in DCR's financial statements.

5. Payments in Bitcoin

Subject to managing the risks associated with bitcoin, it provides an appropriate means of paying the fee of €/£ 500,000 due to Mbuntu's agent.

6. Evaluation of Shirt Manufacturer Deals

DCR should negotiate with O'Neill's and Kappa and request a final bid from both companies.

7. Data Analysis and Data Analytics

A significant amount of work is required to analyse DCR's data and to identify how this data can be utilised. Details of this work are set out in this report.

8. Evaluating DCR's Corporate Social Responsibility (CSR) Strategy

This report identifies the four pillars of CSR, and outlines suggestions for CSR initiatives that could be implemented by DCR.

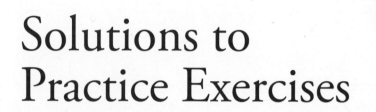

Solutions to
Practice Exercises

Solutions to Practice Exercises

As outlined in **Chapter 4**, FAE case studies are structured around indicators (directed and, sometimes, implicit). However, it is important to remember that the structure of your solution **does not** have to mirror that of the suggested solution.* If you group the indicators together differently, this does not matter; the key point is that you recognise the relevant issues and deal with them appropriately in your answer. This point is often misunderstood by FAE candidates and can lead to unnecessary stress and worry in the exam.

Chapter 4

Practice Exercise 4.1 – Identify Issues to Avoid

In the Dublin City Rovers case (**Supplement A**), the following sentence appears in the last paragraph of the information relating to the stadium tour opportunity: "If we did decide to go it alone, it wouldn't be necessary to consider how the capital expenditure would be funded."

This is a clear instruction – consideration of how any capital expenditure requirements should be funded is not necessary. Therefore, time need not be wasted by thinking about this aspect.

Chapter 5

Practice Exercise 5.1 – Linking the Case Information to the Primary Indicators

Using the directed indicators identified in **Example 4.1**, the Dublin City Rovers case (**Supplement A**), the information required to address the primary indicators is highlighted and underlined below.

Directed Indicator 1 – Accounting treatment of Aviva Stadium lease

At the end of the section on the Aviva Stadium:

> "… I have set out all the details of the Aviva Stadium arrangement in this document [see Appendix I]."

All of the information provided in **Appendix I** will be required to address this primary indicator.

Directed Indicator 2 – Stadium tours evaluation and assessment

In the section entitled 'Opportunity – Aviva Stadium Tours':

> "Given the fact that we will have home matches every other week, the other two bodies are now keen to develop this stadium tour opportunity. Revenue and operating costs would be split three ways. The FAI and IRFU

---

* The solutions outlined here refer specifically to the 2019/2020 examinations and so may differ in terms of technical content.

have a contact with a very experienced events management company, which would manage the running of tours. There is disagreement among our board, however. Half the board members feel that the FAI and IRFU are dependent on us to deliver the footfall, and believe that we should go it alone. These members point to the fact that, unlike domestic football, the playing season for rugby and international football is not consistent. They feel further justified in their view as the FAI and IRFU are prepared to shoulder the development costs to put a walkway and viewing point on the roof and other renovations to create a bespoke visitor centre. For our board meeting next week I said I would take some advice and consider the two options – (a) a joint venture; or (b) going it alone – using strategic decision-making criteria. In the meantime I spoke with a peer in the GAA, which operates a similar model in-house at Croke Park. It receives 150,000 visitors per year; at an average gross revenue per head of €/£ 30. Operating costs associated with running it are €/£ 12 per head. The FAI and IRFU have quietly indicated that the expected operating cost will be around €/£ 6 per head, including the event company's fee. Will you analyse this based on suitability, acceptability and feasibility criteria? I intend to bring a recommendation to the board. Jack's view, for what it's worth, is that we should collaborate with our landlords. If we did decide to go it alone, it wouldn't be necessary to consider how the capital expenditure would be funded."'

Directed Indicator 3 – Risk Register

In the section entitled 'Risk Register':

'Bill changes the conversation now and smiles. "This will sound paradoxical, but you know that we were under enormous pressure over the past couple of years, and we neglected to keep the risk register up to date." Mary sympathises with Bill, but reminds him of the importance of such a document. Bill is pleased to hear Mary's comments recognising the risk register's importance and asks her to prepare a note to remind the board of its obligations in this regard. Bill continues, "I have taken the time to highlight some of the risks I see facing DCR" and passes a sheet of paper across the desk [see Appendix II]."'

All of the information provided in **Appendix II** will be required to address this primary indicator.

Directed Indicator 4 – Accounting treatment of new signing

In the section 'New Signing':

'Bill changes subject now and wishes to talk about an exciting announcement that will be made in the coming days. Jack has persuaded the up-and-coming Zambian footballer, Mbuntu, to join DCR on a four-year deal. Mary is impressed, recalling Mbuntu's recent performances at the Africa Cup of Nations tournament, where he displayed great maturity and leadership for a 17-year-old midfielder. Bill quickly gets into specifics: "Jack was in Zambia on business and he found out that Mbuntu, whose parents and grandparents were educated by Irish missionaries, has a great affection for Ireland and always wanted to come to Ireland. On 1 April 2018, Jack met Mbuntu and his agent and they shook hands on a deal to play for DCR for a four-year period, subject to Mbuntu passing a medical.

"This medical was successfully completed on 30 June 2019. On the same date DCR paid €/£ 5,000 to Mbuntu's Zambian club, Zesco United, for the formal transfer of the player's registration rights to DCR. In addition, DCR have agreed to pay a €/£ 2 million signing-on fee to Zesco United as well as a €/£ 500,000 payment to Mbuntu's agent, Fleecie. Both of these amounts are expected to be paid in the coming weeks. It is also my understanding that Zesco United is now obliged to pay a fee of €/£ 100,000 to Mbuntu's childhood football club, Nchanga United, in relation to this subsequent sale of Mbuntu.

"The representatives of DCR and Mbuntu's agent have agreed that the player will be paid an annual salary of €/£ 1.5 million. An upfront signing-on bonus of €/£ 250,000 for the player was also agreed, subject to Mbuntu completing his four-year contract with DCR. This bonus was paid by DCR on 30 June 2019.'"

Directed Indicator 5 – Payment of agent's fee

In the section 'Agent's Fee':

'Bill continues, "Jack observed that Mbuntu's agent, Fleecie, is a colourful character to say the least. He kept trying to change the terms of the deal. Mbuntu had to instruct him to leave the meeting at one point. Anyway, Fleecie is continuing his antics with an unusual request." Bill pauses, and Mary encourages him to continue. "Fleecie is demanding that his fee of €/£ 500,000 is paid in bitcoin. Now, I have checked and the currency of Zambia is not bitcoin, it is the Zambian kwacha, although US dollars are also widely accepted.'"

Directed Indicator 6 – Negotiation of merchandising deal

In the section 'Negotiation':

'A relieved Bill thanks Mary and moves onto his next point. He wishes to discuss a merchandising contract that has come up for renewal. Bill continues the conversation: "This is one of the things that DCR as a brand has managed to get right. We sell a lot of jerseys, hats and scarves every year. We have always kept our manufacturing supplier local to us, so it was a good media story when the economy was in recession a few years back. Now though, we have outgrown the local supplier's capacity – last year we sold close to 25,000 shirts, which meant we had to order 5,000 shirts each from O'Neills and Kappa. Both companies are competing for our business. Here are the details of their offers [see Appendix III].

What I would like you to do is review the offers and detail for me how we can close-out the negotiations to our advantage. This deal is just for the rights to supply the team and sell DCR shirts and other merchandise. To be clear, Jack will be putting the Goohui logo on the front of the shirts, considering he owns the club!'"

In addition, all of the information provided in **Appendix III** will be required to address this primary indicator.

Directed Indicator 7 – Customer insights and data analytics

In the 'Introduction and Background', the following information is given:

"'DCR enjoyed unprecedented goodwill from the Irish public. However, our original ground was too small, with a capacity of only 2,500 seats, so the ground quickly became untenable and DCR terminated its lease and vacated the ground in the 2014/15 season. The plan to build a state of the art stadium never materialised. Dubbed the 'Dublin City Ramblers' by media and fans, until January 2019 DCR was renting out grounds all over the country for home matches on a one-off rental per match. For example, when DCR drew Manchester United in the third round of the FA Cup a few years' back, DCR cut a deal with the GAA (Gaelic Athletic Association) to rent its flagship stadium, Croke Park, for the home fixture; it was a complete sell out of 82,000 seats. By comparison, when DCR played Rotherham FC back in October 2018, Dalymount Park, with a capacity of 4,300, was rented. This unsatisfactory arrangement has tested relations with ardent fans who have stuck with DCR through thick and thin. DCR has also been dogged by unsympathetic journalists all too eager to use the lack of a permanent home as a stick to beat the club's management with."

And, in 'The Aviva Stadium' section:

"'In January 2019 we struck a deal with the FAI (Football Association of Ireland) and the IRFU (Irish Rugby Football Union). They needed an anchor tenant to guarantee them a regular income, and as we are in the same business we have agreed flexibility where possible. There is good synchronisation between national and domestic football fixtures. There are potentially some clashes in March, with the Rugby Six Nations tournament where we potentially clash on three dates. However, both sporting codes and broadcasters have tremendous sway in re-arranging fixtures in a satisfactory manner. It is working out well and since we moved in average attendance over the last 10 home matches is 40,500. I have set out all the details of the Aviva Stadium arrangement in this document [see **Appendix I**]. We have not reflected the new arrangement in the year-end accounts so I would appreciate it if you could review the file and advise on the appropriate accounting treatment for this deal.'"

In the section entitled 'Customer Insights', the following information on the turnstile data is given:

'Bill thanks Mary for her willingness to address all the issues presented thus far, and says he has only one or two matters left. "Jack is very keen to understand our fan base. He was talking about fantastical software that he uses to analyse data to reveal insights. All very well I told him, but our systems are old and disparate; I don't believe he can get anything of any use from them. We did have to install barcode scanners a number of years ago, for when fans go through the turnstiles, to comply with FIFA directives that all matches are seated. The barcode scanners are mobile units, because we used grounds all over the country."

Mary enquires where this data from the turnstiles might be located. "One of Jack's guys took it off me last week; he said something about a data exercise, whatever that means. He claims to have fixed the data and sent me on a bunch of numbers and a couple of diagrams. I don't know if anyone has done anything with this information. We certainly have not discussed it at board level. You are welcome to look at them." Bill hands Mary a sheet of paper [see Appendix IV] and asks, "Mary, can you help me understand the value of this data? And what steps are involved in a data exercise anyway? I'd appreciate any comments and insights you might have." Mary nods enthusiastically and tells Bill she will have a look at it and give him some analysis.'

In addition, all of the information provided in **Appendix IV** should be noted and linked to this primary indicator.

Directed Indicator 8 – Corporate Social Responsibility

In the section 'Corporate Social Responsibility':

'Bill gratefully hands over the server box and remarks that he has one final issue to discuss. "Mary, I would like you to give some thought to the CSR section of our upcoming annual report. I know we are a while away from having the year-end accounts finalised. In the past we have traditionally paid lip service to this section of the report, with the inclusion of all sorts of inspirational pictures and content. Jack is keen to demonstrate his commitment to the club and would like to use this section of the report as a means of kick-starting any initiatives that we might like to include."'

Chapter 10

Practice Exercise 10.1 – Evaluation of Merchandising Offers

In the Dublin City Rovers case, analysis of the figures in Appendix III results in an NPV of €/£ 2.655 million for both O'Neill's and Kappa. The offers should then be compared using other criteria. On this analysis it is decided that both companies should be invited to submit final bids.

Chapter 11

Practice Exercise 11.1 – Outsourcing Proposal

Outsourcing has significant consequences for the **division that has been manufacturing the component**. Employees in that division may lose their livelihoods, which gives rise to moral and ethical issues. Perhaps, however, there will be opportunities for redeployment to reduce the incidence of redundancies. There will also be a loss of skills, many of which will have been nurtured in the company over a significant time period.

Outsourcing also has implications for the **division that uses the component**. Quality control issues may arise, as the external supplier may fail to meet the company's technical specifications. Also, the external supplier may be servicing the needs of many other customers. This could result in a poorer than expected level of service and there may be delays in the delivery of the outsourced component. The bottom line is that outsourcing will result in a loss of control over the supply of the component.

There may also be implications for the company's **storage and distribution** systems. It may be necessary to carry higher inventories of finished goods, as a contingency against a possible failure by the external supplier to deliver the component on schedule.

From the **overall perspective of the company**, outsourcing will reduce overhead costs and allow more focus on the company's core activities. The closure of the manufacturing division will give rise to significant legal and human resource issues. It will be critical that efficient channels of communication are established with the outsourcing provider and that the provider is monitored as to its financial solvency. It is also vital that a company's goals and strategy are aligned with the objectives of outsourcing.

Analysis The above solution evaluates outsourcing on a cradle-to-grave basis. The implications are considered sequentially for the various stages of the company's operations.

Practice Exercise 11.2 – Proposed Takeover

Proposed Takeover Clearly, the chief executive is in favour of the takeover as he stands to benefit significantly from the deal. From the shareholders' perspective, however, the offer price must be considered in the context of the value of the company's shares. A number of valuation techniques can be employed for this purpose.

The takeover also has implications for the company's workforce, whose employment may not be guaranteed by the new owners. A redundancy package will have to be provided for those employees whose contracts will be terminated. Suppliers may also be at risk, as the new owners may decide to source their supplies elsewhere. Rhyme's customers may also be affected as the new owners may decide to discontinue the supply of certain products.

In the event that the bid is **not** completed, this may have implications for staff morale and for the continuation of the chief executive in his current position.

Profit Maximisation Strategy The proposed profit maximisation strategy may increase the likelihood of the takeover being completed. This depends, however, on the measures being accepted by the company's auditors. Also, changes in accounting policy must be clearly signalled in the financial statements, thus identifying one of the reasons why profit is higher. Further evidence of the strategy may also be unearthed by the bidder at the due diligence stage of the takeover, potentially endangering the completion of the deal.

From the shareholders' perspective, the profit maximisation strategy has other potential disadvantages:

- a higher tax charge;
- higher management remuneration (if bonuses are based on profits); and
- it may be necessary to repeat this profit performance in the next period if the company is still being showcased.

Analysis The solution examines the consequences of the takeover from the perspective of Rhyme Limited's shareholders, its employees and also the company's suppliers.

The implications of the chief executive's profit maximisation strategy are then considered from the perspective of the shareholders, the company's auditors and the party bidding for the company's shares.

The solution to **Practice Exercise 11.2** illustrates how an issue can be explored by considering the conflicting interests and perspective of different stakeholders in Rhyme Limited.

Practice Exercise 11.3 – Establishing Links

Morse Limited has an imbalance in its corporate governance structure. The board currently comprises skilled craftsmen whose primary focus is on the quality of the company's fireplaces. As a consequence, Morse Limited has made no effort to research changing consumer preferences. Perhaps customers are now more concerned about fashion and price than about ensuring that they get a fireplace which is of top-notch quality.

It is vital that Morse Limited's corporate governance structure be overhauled. The company should appoint board members who have financial and marketing expertise. This will facilitate Morse's development of a business strategy that will enable them to compete more effectively in the changing fireplace market.

Analysis It is clear that Morse Limited has serious flaws in its corporate governance structure. This has resulted in a business strategy that focuses exclusively on quality while completely ignoring issues of style and pricing. The inevitable consequence has been a decline in the company's sales.

This solution has established a link between Morse's corporate governance structure and its business strategy. This, in turn, identifies a further linkage between the company's strategy and its sales figures. Thus, an overall link has been established between three business disciplines: corporate governance, business strategy and marketing.

Chapter 12

Practice Exercise 12.1 – Accounting Policy Choice

IAS 40 *Investment Property* permits an entity to choose either a cost model or a valuation model for investment property. Whichever model is chosen will apply to all of an entity's investment properties.

If Jupiter opts for the **cost model**, its investment property will be accounted for under the rules of IAS 16 *Property, Plant and Equipment*. The buildings' portion of the property would therefore be subject to annual depreciation over its estimated useful life.

Should Jupiter opt for the **fair value model**, the investment property will be accounted for under the rules of IAS 40 *Investment Property*. Periodic depreciation would not be charged, and any changes in value of the property would be recorded in profit or loss. Any gain on the property would be subject to capital gains tax, but this is not levied until the asset is sold. Therefore, the choice of policy, whether cost or fair value, will have no effect on the company's tax liability.

Use of the fair value model could result in significant fluctuations in Jupiter's annual profit. Management bonuses, which are currently linked to performance, would then also be affected by property price movements. As these are outside of management's control, a fall in property prices could adversely affect management morale and incentive levels.

Recommendation Jupiter operates a management bonus scheme, which is based on the company's annual profit. It is recommended that Jupiter use the cost model for investment property as permitted by IAS 40 *Investment Property*. This will avoid managerial bonuses being affected by property price movements over which management has no control.

Alternatively, the bonus schemes should be amended to exclude the effect of any valuation adjustments relating to investment property. In this event, the choice between fair value and cost models will have no significant implications, and Jupiter can opt for either policy.

Analysis This answer has employed what is broadly a cradle-to-grave approach. First, it outlines the rules pertaining to accounting policy choice. It relates the choice to the company's circumstances, provides a recommendation, and outlines the implications as follows:
■ authoritative guidance is provided by reference to IAS 40 *Investment Property*;
■ the alternatives (fair value or cost) are evaluated in the context of the specific circumstances of the company;
■ a recommendation is provided; and
■ the implications of that recommendation are outlined.